Making the Budget Process Work

David J. Berg, Gerald M. Skogley, *Editors*

NEW DIRECTIONS FOR HIGHER EDUCATION
MARTIN KRAMER, *Editor-in-Chief*

Number 52, September 1985

Paperback sourcebooks in
The Jossey-Bass Higher Education Series

Jossey-Bass Inc., Publishers
San Francisco • London

David J. Berg, Gerald M. Skogley (Eds.).
Making the Budget Process Work.
New Directions for Higher Education, no. 52.
Volume XIII, no. 4.
San Francisco: Jossey-Bass, 1985.

New Directions for Higher Education
Martin Kramer, *Editor-in-Chief*

New Directions for Higher Education, is published quarterly
by Jossey-Bass Inc., Publishers (publication number USPS
990-880). *New Directions* is numbered sequentially—please
order extra copies by sequential number. The volume and issue
numbers above are included for the convenience of libraries.
Second-class postage rates paid at San Francisco, California,
and at additional mailing offices.

Correspondence:
Subscriptions, single-issue orders, change of address notices,
undelivered copies, and other correspondence should be sent
to Subscriptions, Jossey-Bass Inc., Publishers, 433 California Street,
San Francisco, California 94104.

Editorial correspondence should be sent to Martin Kramer,
2807 Shasta Road, Berkeley, California 94708.

Library of Congress Catalog Card Number 85-60831

International Standard Serial Number ISSN 0271-0560

International Standard Book Number ISBN 87589-750-9

Cover art by WILLI BAUM

Manufactured in the United States of America

Ordering Information

The paperback sourcebooks listed below are published quarterly and can be ordered either by subscription or single-copy.

Subscriptions cost $40.00 per year for institutions, agencies, and libraries. Individuals can subscribe at the special rate of $30.00 per year *if payment is by personal check.* (Note that the full rate of $40.00 applies if payment is by institutional check, even if the subscription is designated for an individual.) Standing orders are accepted.

Single copies are available at $9.95 when payment accompanies order, and *all single-copy orders under $25.00 must include payment.* (California, New Jersey, New York, and Washington, D.C., residents please include appropriate sales tax.) For billed orders, cost per copy is $9.95 plus postage and handling. (Prices subject to change without notice.)

Bulk orders (ten or more copies) of any individual sourcebook are available at the following discounted prices: 10–49 copies, $8.95 each; 50–100 copies, $7.96 each; over 100 copies, *inquire.* Sales tax and postage and handling charges apply as for single copy orders.

To ensure correct and prompt delivery, all orders must give either the *name of an individual* or an *official purchase order number.* Please submit your order as follows:

> *Subscriptions:* specify series and year subscription is to begin.
> *Single Copies:* specify sourcebook code (such as, HE1) and first two words of title.

Mail orders for United States and Possessions, Latin America, Canada, Japan, Australia, and New Zealand to:
> Jossey-Bass Inc., Publishers
> 433 California Street
> San Francisco, California 94104

Mail orders for all other parts of the world to:
> Jossey-Bass Limited
> 28 Banner Street
> London EC1Y 8QE

New Directions for Higher Education Series
Martin Kramer, *Editor-in-Chief*

Contents

Editors' Notes

Making the budget process work has different connotations in different budgetary environments. In the higher education environment, it has different meanings depending on the type of institution, its organizational structure, its governance, its source of revenue, and other important structural considerations.

The budget process has evolved in higher education over a long period of time. Prior to the 1950s when there were fewer students attending higher education institutions, budgeting was a relatively simple process. It was almost always incremental and had very little relationship to numbers of students, specific program offerings, or organizational structure. It was not without form but was utilized more as a one-year plan rather than a long-term commitment to predetermined education objectives.

The early budget documents were designed more to determine overall expenditure by category of expense and income rather than by program offering or organizational structure. With increased numbers of students, new programs, and new sources of support (such as the federal government), accountability became a byword requiring additional planning and more careful allocation of resources.

The large increase in numbers of students also required a process, at least in public institutions, for more equitable allocation of resources to institutions. Due to this need, higher education began using formulas to ensure a more equitable allocation process. Formulas were almost exclusively enrollment driven. They were most often developed with variances for the level of the student (lower division, upper division, graduate, and so on). Formula budgeting accomplished many of the purposes for which it was developed. Formula budgeting also created many additional problems for higher education.

One of the early problems with formula budgeting was the misunderstanding of the purpose of the formula by many of those affected by the process. Too often the formula was interpreted as an allocation process rather than a resource document that was used to receive funds in an equitable manner from funding sources. At best, formulas were an averaging process and could not effectively be understood if the details necessary to meet every allocation test were

1

included in the request document. The result of this fault was to create distrust among administrators, faculty, legislators, and even students who were affected by the budgeting process.

Another of the problems with formula budgeting was the difficulty encountered when reductions in the number of students required a reduction in spending without any relationship to need for the program, marginal spending requirements, or long-term implications of the reduction. Many schools were faced with massive staff reductions, much deferred maintenance, and other long-term problems that had not been considered because the reductions were not planned or there was not enough time to implement changes in an organized manner.

These problems along with a need for processes to handle rapid change brought about new ways of budgeting. The chapters in this sourcebook are intended to provide the reader with some of the philosophies and techniques that have been developed to help administrators, faculty, and governing bodies deal with higher education budgeting problems in a better informed and more effective manner.

The five topics covered here are intended to provide some of the current thought about techniques for shaping the budgeting process that were not available in previous periods. Each technique has been used and each has been successful in the administration of the budget process. The chapters are not sequential or coordinated in the approach to budgeting but rather provide various methods of developing budgets or parts of budgets to assist in raising and allocating resources.

In Chapter One, James Hyatt sets the essential context for effective budgeting noting, as noted later in Chapter Four, that a budget that works only reflects a planning process that works and the data and analysis implied by this process. Evaluation of the past budget is an essential part of the end of each planning period and the beginning of the next. Without an understanding of the underlying concepts of the budget cycle, the potential contributions of its participants will often be wasted.

In Chapter Two, Brenda Albright reflects on how to introduce quality incentives in budgeting and deals with a process developed in the state of Tennessee to change from a typical formula-based system to one that places emphasis on instructional excellence rather than simply numbers of students in various programs. This was accomplished by utilizing input from the people administering the various programs and provided an incentive to the individuals involved rather than the disincentive to quality when merely numbers produced dollars. Some seminal ideas about future opportunities to innovate are also presented and the extremely important concept of performance contracts is discussed.

In Chapter Three, Gene Kemper presents a process developed by one institution to justify and allocate faculty based on an approach developed from the bottom up and verified by comparison with a group of institutions of comparable size in another region of the country. The emphasis of this process was on permitting the allocation of faculty to meet the needs as perceived by the department concerned without allowing outside pressure to determine what was necessary. The follow-up to the justifying need was to defend that need to the governing board and the legislature that provided the funding. This was of particular importance when changing from the traditional formula approach to funding faculty while in a stable or potentially declining enrollment period.

Chapter Four provides a review of the way in which one institution initiated a new budgeting process that involved all of those directly responsible for the implementation and carrying out of the mission of the institution. Since the institution is relatively small, the involvement of those concerned brings about a collegiality that permits a focus on the mission of the institution and a coordinated implementation of the strategy in the long-range plan. While strategic management in a decentralized system as described in this chapter by John Green and David Monical may present problems for larger institutions, it can provide a form of consensus planning and budgeting that is highly desirable for those at smaller institutions.

In Chapter Five, David Berg presents a friendly summary of the current trend toward incentive budget techniques, decontrol, and decentralization. The use of market economy techniques in the nonprofit sector has come to be one of the more exciting trends in higher education planning and budgeting; every active budgeter should be considering incentive issues.

David J. Berg
Gerald M. Skogley
Editors

David J. Berg is assistant vice-president for management planning and information services in the University of Minnesota system.

Gerald M. Skogley is business manager of The Bush Foundation and formerly vice-president for business and finance at the University of North Dakota.

The budget must also act as a plan for generating revenues.

Information: Setting the Context for Effective Budgeting

James A. Hyatt

Effective budgeting is dependent on timely, relevant, and accurate information. Information used in developing the budget should encompass more than current data or future estimates of expenditures and revenues. It should also include an assessment of existing academic and support programs of the institution and provide guidance as to future challenges, such as enrollment declines, and to future opportunities, such as new program offerings and new directions for the institution. Budgetary information is therefore concerned with the past, present, and future condition of the institution.

In order to understand the role of information in the budgetary process, it is useful to look at the reasons for which information is collected. From the standpoint of financial management, information is necessary in order to ascertain the institution's needs for funds and possibilities for generating funds to meet these needs. It is also useful in assessing whether funds are used in an efficient and effective manner and, at the conclusion of the budget cycle, in evaluating whether the needs identified at the beginning of the cycle have been met.

D. J. Berg, Gerald M. Skogley (Eds.). *Making the Budget Process Work.* New Directions for Higher Education, no. 52. San Francisco: Jossey-Bass, December 1985.

The purpose of this chapter will be to provide guidance on how information can be used: (1) in setting institutional priorities and identifying the needs for funds; (2) in examining alternatives for generating funds; (3) in developing a plan and budget for using funds; and (4) in evaluating whether the needs of the institution have been met.

Assessing Institutional Needs

Involvement in the budgetary process normally begins with the issuance of budget guidelines. These guidelines reflect the administration's assessment of inflationary trends, enrollment projections, and other factors that can affect future expenditures and revenues. Guidelines also should reflect new program initiatives and a reassessment of current programs.

In order to develop meaningful budget guidelines certain information is required. At the center of any financial guideline or plan is an assessment of need. In the broadest sense, this assessment is reflected in an organization's role and mission statement. A good role and mission statement indicates what the institution views as its primary role (such as the provision of quality instruction, research, and public service programs) and how it plans to fulfill this role (such as maximizing access to the community through an open door policy, or specializing in certain areas, such as health services or foreign languages).

The first step in assessing the need for funds is to understand funding requirements of existing programs. As part of this process, descriptions of the scope and nature of all institutional activities must be prepared. Information used in preparing these descriptions should include: (1) the mode of instruction, such as lecture or lab; (2) the relationship of the activity to other activites of the institution, such as programs that support other areas of the institution, for instance, science programs that are part of pre-med or engineering programs; (3) the resources necessary to conduct the activity, such as personnel, facilities, and equipment; (4) the costs associated with the activity; and (5) student demand or need for the program. Since this assessment of needs establishes the basis on which all planning and budgetary activities are predicated, care should be exercised in order to ensure that estimates of need are realistic and can be supported by evidence. In this regard, information concerning similar programs at comparable institutions can be useful.

While an assessment of program needs is essential to the

development of an institution's budget, other aspects of institutional operations must be considered. Colleges and universities that operate as not-for-profit organizations have a responsibility to ensure that the assets of the institution are expended for the purposes intended and that they are expended in a fiscally responsible manner. This stewardship responsibility should extend beyond the preparation and issuance of financial reports. It also should be reflected in the institution's policies toward the maintenance of facilities and equipment. Adequate facilities and equipment are essential to maintaining quality academic and support programs. Needs in this area must be reflected in an institution's plans and budgets.

Another aspect related to need involves the ability of an institution to take advantage of new opportunities or to meet new challenges. Institutional decision makers, whether they are faculty or staff, have a responsibility to identify ways in which their institution can better respond to current and emerging needs. In this regard, a high degree of institutional flexibility enables an institution to consider new methods of delivering services and alternative ways of funding its activities. Such initiatives, however, should be tempered with an understanding of the environment in which the institution operates. State laws or regulations, for example, may prohibit the institution from engaging in certain activities or taking advantage of alternative funding sources. In addition, institutional policies concerning tenure and the existence of collective bargaining agreements may limit institutional efforts to reallocate resources.

In a less tangible sense, the attitude toward change of the institution's board, senior administrators, faculty, and staff can hamper an effective assessment of need. In this regard, an organization that is concerned with merely maintaining the status quo runs the risk of severely undermining the planning and budgeting process. These activities must not be perceived as mechanical or rote exercises but as a dynamic and interactive process. Adequate funds, for example, must be available to invest in the future. In the profit sector, such a policy involves the use of venture capital or seed money. If new sources of funds are available for this purpose, then the impact on existing programs is minimal. If no new funds are available, then a reallocation of existing resources may be necessary.

While an assessment of need is normally conducted when a new activity or program is proposed, such an assessment should be an integral part of planning and budgeting for all institutional programs. It is better to begin the budgetary process with an assessment of needs rather than have to justify the budget during budget hearings by indicating that "this is the way we have operated in the past." A sound assessment of needs is, therefore, the foundation of effective budgeting.

Generating Funds

The identification of needs is only one aspect of the budget process. Another aspect involves a determination of how these needs can best be met. In order to ascertain whether there are sufficient funds to meet all institutional needs, certain information is required. First, information on the sources of funds allows decision makers to decide among a number of alternatives for generating funds. Funding for institutional activities can come from a variety of sources, including traditional sources of support, new sources of revenue, and reallocation of existing resources to meet priority needs. Traditional sources of support include: tuition and fees; gifts, grants, and contracts; revenues from auxilliary activities, such as housing and food service; endowment income; and, in the case of public institutions, state and local appropriations. Other sources of traditional support can also include contributed services or donated facilities and equipment.

In order to assess whether traditional sources can generate the funds necessary to support existing and proposed programs, it is also necessary to understand some of the factors that limit revenue generation. In the case of tuition and fees, revenue from this source can be affected by market considerations, such as demand for institutional programs and the tuition and fees charged by comparable institutions, and by institutional policies, such as admissions standards and desired faculty-to-student ratios. Other considerations, such as the marginal cost or revenue associated with additional students and the institution's ability to mount effective student recruitment and retention programs, are also critical to an assessment of this source of support.

Similar constraints affect other traditional sources of support, and it is important to recognize these constraints in developing a plan for revenue generation and in building a budget. For example, state and local appropriations can be affected by local and national economic conditions and by the priority of higher education relative to other needs. In a similar manner, income generated by institutional endowments is dependent on market conditions, and support for research and student financial aid programs is dependent on governmental policies and initiatives in these areas.

Because of the constraints on the traditional sources of revenue outlined above, a number of colleges and universities have turned to alternative methods for generating revenue. Such methods include real estate developments, venture capital projects, tax-exempt and nontraditional borrowing arrangements, for-profit subsidiary corporations, partnerships with commercial enterprises, and agreements that provide tax benefits for various types of contributions. Examples of innovative financing methods include joint ventures with industry on real estate developments and the use of short-term, variable rate financing—rather than long-term, fixed-rate bonds.

While a number of alternatives for generating additional funds are attractive, care should be exercised in two areas. First, the expertise and availability of staff at the institution to implement these alternatives should be considered. Second, the amount of risk involved in each of these ventures and the changes in federal regulations governing the use of such alternatives as sale-leaseback and debt financing should be assessed. In both areas an informed decision maker is an institution's best insurance that its assets will be managed and invested in a responsible and judicious manner.

Information useful to assessing alternative strategies for generating funds is available from a number of sources. An excellent study is *Creative Capital Financing for State and Local Governments* (Peterson and Hough, 1983). Several institutions have also found it beneficial to engage outside consultants with expertise in the capital area. Regardless of the method used to evaluate alternatives, it is essential that decision makers match the costs and benefits of these alternatives to the role and mission of their institution.

If sufficient funds cannot be generated from either traditional or new sources, decision makers must consider whether to reallocate funds from existing areas to meet the priorities of their institution. Important elements in developing an effective reallocation process include: (1) faculty and constituent involvement in reallocation, (2) assessment of institutional role and mission, (3) quality of academic and support programs, and (4) long-term versus short-term costs and benefits associated with reallocation (NACUBO, 1982). Information essential to developing reallocation plans can come from institutional program reviews, accreditation reports, and analysis of program costs. A useful source of information on reallocation procedures at five public colleges and universities is *Reallocation: Strategies for Effective Resource Management* (Hyatt, Shulman, and Santiago, 1984).

A solid understanding of the institution's needs for funds and its capability of generating them is the basis on which plans and budgets should be built. While incremental budgeting, or the continuation of existing program expenditures with inflationary adjustments, is by far the most common method of building budgets, it is not responsive to future challenges and opportunities facing an institution. By being cognizant of institutional needs and alternatives for generating funds, participants can influence the budgetary process rather than blindly perpetuating past activities. The information outlined above provides the context in which the plans and budgets of an institution are developed. In this regard, budgets are "the blueprints for the orderly execution of program plans; they serve as control mechanisms to match anticipated and actual revenues and expenditures" (NACUBO, 1982, p. 1).

Using Funds

As noted earlier, involvement in the budgetary process normally begins with the issuance of budget guidelines and ends with the approval of the budget. Budgeting, however, is a dynamic process. Unlike a financial statement, a budget is subject to change. Changes usually occur as a result of over- or under-expenditures of funds or from unrealized or excess revenues. Thus, an informed participant must understand the dynamics associated with the use of funds.

In order to understand how budgets are implemented, it is necessary to understand three aspects of the implementation process: (1) how budgets are controlled; (2) how budgets are monitored; and (3) how budgets are adjusted.

Budgetary controls are used to ensure that funds are expended for the purpose intended and that all expenditures are in compliance with institutional policies and procedures. Controls, for example, can relate to purchases of equipment, travel by faculty and staff, and recruitment and dismissal of personnel. In addition, the transfer of funds between various expenditure categories within the budget, such as from salary and wages to travel or equipment, is also controlled centrally by the budget or business office. The purpose of these controls is to ensure that all units comply with the institution's plan of action as set forth in the budget.

A second aspect related to the implementation of the budget involves the monitoring of revenues and expenditures. Information pertaining to this area is normally available through budget variance reports. Budget variance reports provide comparisons between amounts budgeted for an activity and actual expenditures and revenues. Depending on an institution's particular budget procedure, variance reports are prepared either monthly, quarterly, or semian-nually. These reports enable administrators to identify problem areas and make the necessary adjustments to bring the budget into balance. While budget variance reports primarily focus on the expen-diture of funds, an informed administrator should also examine the relationship of projected revenues to actual funds received. As noted earlier, revenues are an important part of the budgetary equation and due diligence must be exercised in order to ensure that sufficient funds are available to meet institutional needs. Information related to revenue production can come from a variety of sources within the institution. Information on enrollments collected by the registrar's office, for example, is used to estimate tuition and fee revenue. In a similar manner, information pertaining to other revenue sources can come from: the treasurer's office; auxiliary service operations, such as housing and food service; the development office; and the grant and contract office. Since the source of this information is so diverse, good communication within the institution is essential to the monitoring of revenue production and to the implementation of the budget.

While it is important to understand the policies and proce-dures that control the expenditures of funds and how to monitor expenditures and revenues, it is essential that the process for adjust-ing the budget be clearly understood. Adjustments for over expen-ditures are normally handled through budget revisions. Assignment of responsibility, designation of authority, and procedures for budget revisions should be documented and approved by the governing board of the institution. If the amount of the adjustment can be accommodated within the existing budget by transferring funds from one budget account to another, the chief executive officer usu-ally has authority to approve such adjustments. If, however, the amounts involved are large enough to change the anticipated net results of the original budget, the governing board should give for-mal approval before increased expenditures are authorized.

The need for budget adjustments is sometimes accommodated through the use of contingency funds or reserves. While the existence of such funds provides some stability to institutional operations, due care should be exercised to ensure that such funds are not used for purposes that alter the intent or purpose of the original budget. Contingency plans should also be prepared prior to the implemen-tation of the budget, so that institutional operations can proceed in an orderly and coordinated fashion.

While the literature on budgeting has traditionally focused on how to prepare a budget, the manner in which the budget is implemented can be of equal or greater importance. It is important, therefore, that those individuals charged with developing the budget follow through on their responsibilities by ensuring that: (1) expenditures and revenues are subject to controls that reflect institutional policies and procedures; (2) that expenditures and revenues are monitored to ensure compliance with the budget; and (3) that budget adjustments are made in conformance with the intent of the original budget.

Evaluation

Since budgets are frequently developed from historical revenue and expenditure information, it is important that a thorough review process be conducted at the conclusion of the budget cycle. Such a review provides valuable information for those charged with developing future budgets. In order to provide a comprehensive assessment of the budget, the review should focus on the following areas: (1) budget versus actual expenditures and revenues during the budget process, (2) budget revisions, and (3) achievement of goals during the period.

An analysis of budgeted versus actual expenditures and revenues should identify areas in which variations from the budget occured and the reasons for these variances. Such an evaluation helps to refine and improve future revenue and expenditure forecasts and provides guidance in assessing future needs. In this regard, the budget process is cyclical in that the development of future budgets is dependent on a prompt and comprehensive assessment of past performance.

As noted earlier, budget revisions or adjustments are made during the budget cycle in order to bring the budget into balance with actual revenue and expenditure patterns. A clear understanding of the use of and rationale for these revisions, however, can help in evaluating institutional performance and assessing the impact of these revisions on future budgets. A budget revision, for example, may result from increased utility expenditures resulting from severe weather conditions. In this instance, the impact of the revision on future budgets may be difficult to predict since it resulted from factors not under institutional control. Another revision, however, may involve the hiring of an additional faculty member, which could result in a recurring commitment of funds in future budgets.

Since budgets are developed from an assessment of institutional needs and are predicated on a set of goals and objectives for the institution, an important element of the review process is an assessment of whether these goals and objectives have been met. For example, has program enrollment met expectations or have services prescribed in the budget been provided? The results of this review process provide valuable information for future planning and budgeting activities.

Conclusion

The budget process can only be effective if participants are in possession of timely, relevant, and accurate information. In order to assess what information meets these criteria, it is important that the dynamics of the budget process be understood. As in any organization, the budget and planning process at a college or university should begin with an assessment of institutional needs. The focal point of this assessment is the role and mission statement of the institution. Following an assessment of needs, an evaluation of funding sources to meet these needs must be conducted. During this process the potential and constraints associated with each source of support (traditional, nontraditional, and reallocated) should be considered. Once the needs for funds and sources of funds have been identified, the budget can be developed. Information, therefore, is vital for effective budgeting.

Budgeting should involve more than the issuance of budget guidelines and preparation of the budget. Interested parties must also understand the process whereby the budget is implemented and how to evaluate institutional performance following the budget period. Such information contributes to the accuracy and relevance of future budgets. Information on institutional performance relative to the budget enables an institution to identify problem areas as well as areas of future opportunities. In order to take an active role in budgeting, one must look beyond the budget document itself to the factors that govern its development, implementation, control, and evaluation.

References

National Association of College and University Business Officers (NACUBO). *College and University Business Administration*. Washington, D.C.: NACUBO, 1982.

Hyatt, J. A., Shulman, C. H., and Santiago, A. A. *Reallocation: Strategies for Effective Resource Management*. Washington, D.C.: NACUBO, 1984.

Peterson, J. E., and Hough, W. C. *Creative Capital Financing for State and Local Governments*. Chicago, Ill.: Municipal Finance Officers Association of the United States and Canada, 1983.

James A. Hyatt is director of the Financial Management Center of the National Association of College and University Business Officers.

*If budget policy accentuates learning, instructional
excellence is more easily attainable.*

Quality Incentives
in the Budget

Brenda N. Albright

Those of us at the state level frequently receive inquiries from faculty
and administrators concerning budget policy and its effect on institutions' funding and educational policies. A president asks, "If we
lose fifty FTEs, will we lose funds? If we enroll more students in the
fall will we gain?" A university professor asks, "Why are only 40
percent of freshmen placed in developmental mathematics courses
when placement tests indicate that 80 percent should be? Will the
institution lose funds if we place students in remedial courses? Is
state budget policy forcing institutions to ignore student needs?"
Another professor asks, "Why am I being encouraged by the dean
to enroll students for at least fifteen student credit hours when the
student cannot successfully carry the load? Is student load related
to funding? Will my institution or department lose funds if I don't
follow this practice?"

From these and similar questions one concludes that not
only are we in higher education obsessed with losing funds but
many if not most higher education administrators and faculty lack
an understanding of how the budget process works at the state,
institutional, and departmental levels and what the budget policies

D. J. Berg, Gerald M. Skogley (Eds.). *Making the Budget Process Work.* New Directions for
Higher Education, no. 52. San Francisco: Jossey-Bass, December 1985.

are. Conversely, when educational and budgeting policies and practices are reviewed in tandem, one concludes that most state-level policy is not sensitive to, and budget makers do not fully comprehend, the effect of the budget on institutional policies and attitudes toward critical instructional issues.

Not only is the budget the primary instrument that a state uses to implement public policy, it is also a reflection of larger societal movements and public values. Since budget policies, whether real or imagined, profoundly affect institutional and individual behaviors, such policies should be periodically reviewed to ascertain their effectiveness in achieving the intended outcomes so that adjustments can be made when contraindications occur. At the state level, enrollment-driven formulas developed during the 1960s reflect the value placed by society on equity, fairness, and social justice. Institutions were encouraged to provide greater access, and the financial rewards were tied to increased numbers of students. These policies were successful in achieving the desired outcome—greater access. However in most cases, instructional standards declined along with achievement of this goal. Similarly, salary policies have successfully encouraged faculty to achieve individual and institutional recognition through research and publishing, but where faculty priorities and energies have been diverted from teaching, these policies have also been detrimental to achieving excellence. While enrollment-driven formulas and institutional salary policies are the two most frequently cited budgetary factors affecting institutional behavior during the past two decades, policies in other areas, such as remediation, have also significantly altered the instructional process. The budget policies of the past have proven to be extremely effective in changing institutional and individual behaviors.

Quality is the emphasis of the 1980s, and current budget policies are being evaluated to determine if adjustments are needed to reward instructional excellence. Higher education qualitative issues have been addressed in a number of recently completed national studies that focus on recommended improvements for undergraduate instruction. While many study recommendations have no discernible budgetary implications, the budget process, funding policies, and financial requirements exert pressure on virtually all decision processes including instructional quality. This chapter examines recommendations that would improve the quality of undergraduate education and that clearly impinge on the budget at the state and institutional levels. What is the current role of the budget in promoting student learning and development? How can budget policies be changed to foster higher quality learning? What methods of finance are available to states and institutions to meet requirements to fund improved student learning and development?

Role of the Budget in Student Learning and Development

The state and higher education institutions appear to have dichotomous roles in the budget process and differing responsibilities for student learning and development. The state's budget roles are to provide adequate resources, to distribute funds on an equitable basis among institutions, and to promote broad statewide goals such as economic development, access, or quality. The institutional roles are to seek additional resources from the state and from fiscal and academic management. The department is clearly the decision-making unit for instructional qualitative areas including what will be taught, what standards will be maintained, who will be admitted, and who will graduate. There is growing state interest in objective evidence that quality is being maintained or improved (Folger, 1984). While the state and institutional budgeting and instructional processes appear separable, there is considerable evidence that state and institutional budgeting policies and practices affect student learning and development, and many policies need adjusting if they are to be effective in promoting improved student learning. Areas targeted for change include: state and institutional quantitative and nonteaching reward systems, resource allocation policies, and funding adequacy issues.

Quantitative and Nonteaching Reward Systems. With regard to state-level policies, the loudest criticisms are leveled at enrollment-driven formulas that reward quantity over quality. The criticism is that when institutions are funded on the basis of enrollments, they devote their energies to maintaining or increasing enrollments to meet costs and thereby are unable to exert quality control (NIE, 1985). However, the effect of enrollment-driven funding policies on distribution of funds among institutions and among departments is, in large measure, more imagined than real. Most states have policies that separate enrollment and funding so that the distribution of funds among institutions is less sensitive to enrollment change. Enrollment caps, corridors, cushions, marginal, fixed and variable costs, incremental and base budgeting have been incorporated into virtually all budgetary systems and are clearly evident in numerical analyses of institutional costs per student and discipline unit costs. These budget changes do not reward growth, nor do they reward instructional improvement; rather, the effect of these policies is primarily protection of institutions' resource bases. Institutions with declining or stable enrollments and a protected resource base have increased opportunities to reallocate resources for the purpose of enhancing instructional quality. In many respects, the difficulty is not the existence of state-level qualitative reward systems, but rather the absence of state-level quantitative reward systems. While numerous states have considered implementation of instructional performance criteria and instructional outcomes measures in the budgeting system, Tennessee is the only state that uses such criteria to allocate a portion of state funds among institutions. The pervasive trend of deemphasizing enrollment in the state budgeting system however, establishes a more conducive environment for the development of quality-related changes (outlined in a subsequent section).

Enrollment-related incentive structures have also encouraged institutions to provide high school-level courses so that the volume of college remedial activity is substantial. This trend of lowering standards has been exacerbated by state-level policies regarding remediation. A number of states have adopted policies to assign the responsibility for teaching basic skills to high schools, not colleges or universities, and these policies have been underscored by higher education budget practices that fund only degree-credit courses. The effect on institutional behavior is predictable—remedial courses are reclassified to degree-credit courses. Although "research suggests that students may actually learn more from such courses if they are offered for credit" (NIE, 1984, p. 49), by not separately identifying and funding these programs, states have in some instances inhibited instructional improvement, and most states cannot identify either how much remedial education there is or how effective the programs are. While states have stiffened high school graduation standards, implemented competency testing for high school graduates, and increased the number of required academic courses for college admission, the future portends remediation for students who graduated in the prereform period, reentry students, and other students who lack basic skills. The prevailing views are that institutions should offer remedial courses when necessary; that students enrolled in such programs should carry limited course loads (NIE, 1984); and that since remedial offerings cut into the college curriculum and reduce the amount of college-level coursework, they should be reduced when possible (Bennett, 1984).

Involvement in Learning (NIE, 1984) recommends an environment wherein institutions are not competing with one another for limited resources but rather competing for the best ideas and programs to advance student learning, and program improvement funds are recommended to inject an element of quality into the system. Most states have budgetary components that direct funding categorically to various programs; however, these approaches are not typically designed as instructional outcomes reward systems but rather as resource input enhancements. Some states have adopted centers-of-excellence programs; although these programs have performance-based criteria, they frequently are research rather than instructional centers.

At the institutional level, increasing the importance given to teaching in the processes of hiring, tenure, promotion, and compensation as well as assessment of teacher effectiveness are recommended to improve instructional improvement (NIE, 1984; AAC, 1985; Bennett, 1984). While a number of states and school systems have recently adopted merit pay systems at the elementary and secondary levels, the implementation of teaching-oriented reward systems at the collegiate level, while feasible, is not evident.

Resource Allocation. Recent reports are critical of the allocation of resources at both the state and institutional level. Funding formulas in most states recognize differential institutional funding practices by course level whereby upper-level courses are funded on the average about 50 percent higher than at the lower level. The differential costs are attributable primarily to two factors: smaller classes and lower faculty teaching loads. They also reflect institutional priorities with regard to research and graduate level instruction with senior-level research faculty assignments at this level.

There has also been a significant shift of students from education and the liberal arts to business, engineering, and more technical fields. It is interesting to note, however, that the shift of institutional resources to these fields has been less dramatic. Institutional funds do not appear to be following the students.

Also, within some states and institutions there have been concerns expressed regarding the significant allocation of resources to noninstructional areas, particularly athletic and building programs. Do these allocations divert instructional funds?

Funding Adequacy. Are funds available to ensure that higher quality instruction is provided? While adequacy of funds does not ensure that qualitative goals will be met, lack of funds may guarantee lack of quality. A complicating factor is that the relationship between quality and funding is not direct, linear, or precise. The loss in faculty purchasing power and the deteriorating physical plant and equipment are factors that may negatively affect students' learning. While most faculties are now experiencing some gain in purchasing power, the shortage and obsolescence of instructional equipment is identified as a major financing issue. Who is responsible for funding adequacy? The state? The institution? The student? How can adequacy be addressed to ensure a more stable funding environment, particularly in states with limited resources?

Recommended Changes for Higher Quality Learning

A number of changes may be implemented by either states or institutions for the purpose of fostering higher quality learning. Similarly, many budgetary incentive systems that have proven successful in one budgeting area, such as research, hold promise for effectiveness in instruction as well. Some changes are process oriented, while others are policy directed.

A Process Change—Multi-Year Funding Contracts. One recommended change is for states and institutions to consider developing multi-year funding contracts with predetermined financial parameters and specific instructional qualitative objectives. States could develop these contracts on an institutional or instructional function basis while institutions might consider contracts for academic departments. Such contracts can ameliorate the uncertainty and anxiety that accompany funding reductions associated with enrollment decline while also providing a more reasonable time frame for implementation and measurement of qualitative improvements. As one institutional vice-president recently stated, "It is difficult to get faculty and staff to talk about instructional improvement when they are uncertain about whether or not they will be here next year." Similarly, states and institutions devote considerable energies to evaluating enrollment changes from year-to-year with the result that efforts and energies are not focused on instructional changes. In most states and institutions the budget cycle is such that the mechanics are emphasized. Typically, states spend the entire year in a series of negotiations over level of funding including hearings with institutions, the governors' staff, and legislators; then the cycle begins again. Little time is available for assessment of program effectiveness. This excessive preoccupation with numbers at the state level elicits a negative response from institutions and faculties (AAC, 1985).

Since most states operate on an annual budget cycle and

since higher education agencies and institutions do not control the purse strings, it can be argued that a multi-year funding approach is too radical. This is particularly so given historical practices, the sensitivity of state tax collections to economic conditions, and the legislature's responsibility for appropriating funds (especially since the composition of the legislature frequently changes with elections). Certainly, universal implementation of this approach at the state level would require the commitment of political as well as higher education leaders. Nonetheless, the multi-year funding approach has been implemented successfully at the state level. In 1983, Tennessee's Governor Lamar Alexander proposed a three-year budget that specified by general state program area the uses of additonal revenue generated from a proposed tax increase. While funding of the program was delayed for one year, the plan has generally been followed for two years, with legislative modifications taking the form of funding for additional programs rather than reductions to the proposed expenditure plan. A more restrictive application of multi-year funding contracts would not necessarily require commitment by state leadership. If the contracts do not require additional funds or if the number of institutions or programs included in the contractual mechanism were limited, then this approach would likely be perceived as a variation of the widely accepted cushioning budgetary techniques.

It is also important to note that concurrent with multi-year funding, the Tennessee legislature took what may be a path-finding step when it enacted the Comprehensive Education Reform Act of 1984, which establishes a number of higher education goals, some of which are related to outcomes (Folger, 1984). Examples of the goals include an improvement in the average National Teacher Exam scores of students enrolled in public university teacher preparation programs and an increase in the number of students from public universities who pass all parts of professional licensing examinations on the first attempt in fields for which a licensure exam is required. The legislation requires that annual benchmarks be established for each institution to evaluate progress toward goals and that a list of achievements be submitted to a Legislative Oversight Committee created to review the effectiveness of the new programs.

The multi-year state budgeting approach and allied performance criteria described for Tennessee could be modified by higher education state agencies and institutions and applied to their funding processes. In some instances, this would forestall implementing such programs externally. While multi-year funding contracts may be most effective in an environment where additional state resources are forthcoming (as is the case in Tennessee), they can also be effective in states with more stable funding environments because of the generalized trend of institutions with declining enrollments. By protecting institutional base-level funding by specifying minimum funding levels, states provide institutions initiate performance contracts that emphasize instructional qualitative factors. A state higher education agency that uses a formula approach could continue to use its formula to distribute funds among institutions but adopt an alternative funding mechanism whereby institutions could select a multi-year performance contract that would guarantee a minimum level of funding (for example, no less than the base year less 5 percent for a three-year period). Such a contract would provide that the institution develop a set of measurable instructional improvement goals, and evaluate, on an annual basis, progress toward achieving them. For states that utilize an incremental budgeting system, this approach could easily be incorporated within the existing budgeting structure. The variations in application of this concept are endless. The possibilities include: mandatory and voluntary institutional participation, application to all or some portion of institutional funding, application to certain types of or all institutions, and so forth. Whatever the variation, this approach can help redirect the budget process at the state and institutional levels from quantitative to qualitative considerations.

Whether or not a state implements multi-year performance contracts, such approaches could be implemented by institutions at the academic department level. In fact, the base protection element of this funding approach has been used by most institutions. Although there have been significant shifts in student enrollments, typically from education and liberal arts to business and engineering, funding for academic colleges and departments with such enrollment drops has been relatively stable, as evidenced by significant increases in unit costs of these departments. The multi-year performance contract approach aids in establishing a relationship between improved resource allocations and instructional goals. In other words, resources, in the form of faculty time or operating expense, are directed toward achieving measurable improvements in teaching rather than being absorbed into the existing departmental system through lighter teaching loads or smaller classes.

In many respects, these recommended changes are built on existing budgeting processes and practices. Base protection is a common procedure used by every state; the change proposed here would make this practice more explicit and specific. By publicly establishing multi-year funding parameters, pressures on institutions and faculties to focus on numbers of students are lessened considerably. Institutions and departments can choose instructional improvement activities. By publicly establishing instructional performance contracts or goals, higher education focuses its energies on appropriate instructional outcomes. In some respects, this approach is like incremental budgeting and could, of course, be easily implemented in a state using this system. The similarity is that it provides base protection and stable funding. It is distinctive from incremental budgeting in performance criteria, the multi-year approach, and the potential applicability to selected institutions within a system. At both the institutional and state levels, multi-year contractual funding approaches lend themselves to selective or pilot implementation and do not require additional resources. Also, they are likely to garner support from faculty in all departments. For faculty in disciplines with declining enrollments, they represent job security. For faculty in disciplines with stable or growing enrollments, they represent accountability. Certain cautions must be considered: if states aim too low in projecting funding parameters, then the self-fulfilling prophecy becomes a constraint, not an opportunity. Conversely, if parameters are set too high, then, like many long-range planning activities, this funding approach becomes a futile exercise. The establishment of a lower-limit funding parameter, however, could bring certainty and funding stability to a number of institutions. What happens if institutions do not succeed in attaining agreed-upon instructional goals? The answer depends greatly on the environment of the state and institution. However, two points should be made. First, the power of the budget in providing performance incentives is formidable. Second, institutions have failed to achieve performance goals in the past, and states and institutions have been successful in developing ways to deal with these situations, though typically after the fact.

Seed Money and Cost Recoveries for Teaching

In addition to implementing changes to salary, hiring, and promotion policies in order to emphasize the importance of teaching, states and institutions should consider other incentives modeled on successful research budgetary reward systems. A number of states and most universities have developed funding policies in the research area that provide incentives for attracting external research funds or rewards for obtaining these funds. At the state level, Tennessee's funding formula, for example, allocates $1 to $1.5 million each year to institutions based on performance as measured by dollar value of research grants. A number of states return all or some portion of indirect cost recovery funds to institutions as a reward for successfully obtaining these funds. Similarly, institutions provide incentives in the form of released time or sabbaticals to promising researchers in the hope of receiving a good return on the institution's investment in the form of additional research grants and contract awards. Another common institutional budgeting practice is to return all, or some portion, of the indirect cost recovery from grants and contracts to the department as a reward for research efforts. In general, these practices are viewed as effective and appropriate budgeting techniques.

The budgeting system now used for research could be adapted to provide an incentive and reward structure for effective teaching. The system could easily be implemented at the institutional level. In the same way that departmental chairmen receive and approve faculty proposals for released time to develop proposals for external research funds, programs could be developed for faculty to apply for released time to improve institutional effectiveness or to reform the curriculum. Similarly, institutions could develop funding approaches analogous to the allocation of indirect cost recoveries by allocating funds to those departments that successfully develop methods of improving instruction. If one of the primary outcomes of improved instruction is higher retention rates, then institutions should have additional resources in the form of student fees, a portion of which could be allocated to departments for discretionary uses such as equipment or other operating expenses. To provide an even stronger incentive, states could establish teaching incentive funds available to institutions or departments on a matching fund basis.

At the state level, techniques that have been successful in providing research incentives and rewards could also be modified for the purpose of improving teaching. Tennessee's instructional evaluation formula component has been widely cited as an approach to allocate state funds on instructional outcomes criteria. Two noteworthy characteristics of the Tennessee approach include the relatively small portion of funds allocated by this factor and the noncompetition for funds among institutions. When the program was first implemented in 1979, less than 2 percent of an institution's state appropriations were allocated based on the instructional evaluation factor; now it is 5 percent. All institutions have implemented instructional assessment systems and have demonstrated considerable progress in attaining instructional outcome goals. Also, there is no competition for funds among institutions. The funding mechanism was designed so that each institution could receive only a specified percent of the statewide instructional evaluation pool of funds by demonstrating success in instructional improvements; the institution is not eligible to receive funds not earned by another institution. Similarly, institutional success in instructional improvement is measured, to some extent, by peer analysis so that community colleges are not competing with comprehensive universities. In essence, if all institutions demonstrate the same rate of progress in instructional improvement this component has no effect on the distribution of funds among institutions.

Frontloading and Two Years of Liberal Education. A frontloading strategy whereby institutions allocate faculty and other resources to increased service to first- and second-year undergraduate students for the purpose of improving student retention is recommended by the NIE study group (NIE, 1984). The report also recommends that states revise funding formulas so that institutions receive as many dollars for a freshman or sophomore as a junior or senior student. While most institutions have had opportunities to make shifts on the basis of discipline and level, they have not chosen to do so. While state budget allocations typically allocate fewer resources to lower than upper level instruction, this allocation is typically based on historical cost studies so that, to the extent that institutions reallocate from upper to lower levels of instruction, this change in funding would likely be reflected in state allocation mechanisms. Institutions in most states have considerable flexibility in the allocation of resources so that there are no restraints prohibiting this practice. In many respects, it would appear that the specter of declining student enrollment combined with enrollment-based funding formulas would encourage institutions to place more faculty at the lower level so that student retention would be improved; however, this has not been the case. Despite precipitous enrollment declines in disciplines such as education, it appears that departmental funding remains stable, and the allocation of resources is enhanced at the upper rather than the lower instructional levels.

While it is difficult to accept the argument that by changing state funding formulas to allocate funds equally to upper and lower levels, instructional improvement will automatically take place, frontloading, by developing and funding more comprehensive remedial education and advising programs, may prove to be extremely effective. Remedial programs, on the average, cost about the same as upper-level instruction. By targeting resources to freshman and sophomore students most in need of instructional assistance, there is a greater likelihood that improved student retention and enhanced access will occur. By developing budgetary and reporting mechanisms that separately fund and monitor postsecondary remediation activities, states may encourage improved learning. Institutions with declining enrollments also have the incentive and resources to implement such programs.

Course requirements have been a central topic in recent national studies that recommend that all bachelor's degree recipients have two full years of liberal education (NIE, 1984), a core of common studies (Bennett, 1984), or a minimum required curriculum (AAC, 1985). Again, the problem is not the presence of budget systems that penalize those institutions that make these academic decisions, but rather the absence of systems that reward such actions. The multi-year funding contracts described earlier may provide an incentive for institutions to be more adventurous in considering alternative academic curricula.

Methods of Finance

It has been recommended that higher education seek to achieve "excellence without extravagance" (NIE, 1984, p. 3). Ironically, no one has recommended that ancillary programs, such as athletics or public service activities, seek success without extravagance. A careful review of expenditures for these ancillary activities may disclose the opportunity to fund incentive programs for instructional quality. For a number of institutions, participation in non-self-supporting athletics programs not only diverts funds from instruction or instructional support areas (when few athletes achieve success as measured by academic program completion) but also damages the institution's academic image. For states and institutions desiring support for instructional improvement, there are several alternatives: quality instruction student fee, endowments, and reallocation. These approaches could be utilized to generate funds that could then be applied to qualitative improvements.

Quality Student Fee. Are students who pay fees to support intercollegiate athletics, to retire indebtedness on the student union building, and so forth, likely to be willing to pay a fee to improve instruction? For more up-to-date equipment? For smaller classes? For more advisers? While these questions have not been placed before students in the form of a referendum, it is ventured that students would support such measures; however, the student consumer would likely expect significant return for this investment.

A fairly modest fee at either a public or private institution, if dedicated to quality instruction, could generate significant new resources. While student fees represent only 25 percent of all educational and general revenue in the public sector, they comprise approximately half of total unrestricted expenditures if allocated exclusively to instruction. A 10 percent increase in student fees (about $100 a year at a university, and $60 a year at a two-year institution), when dedicated to instruction, represents a 5 percent increase, or margin of difference, to the instructional component. While states have not been reluctant to propose such fees for ancillary activities, there appears to be no clear trend in dedicating student fees for qualitative purposes. However, such a proposal merits serious consideration.

Endowments. A number of states have established endowment or trust funds through state appropriations for the purpose of attracting eminent scholars. Virginia has had such a program for approximately twenty years, Florida for six, and a number of states, including Tennessee, have recently begun such programs. One obvious advantage to these programs is their permanence; they are not affected by the whims of students, by legislators, or by governors. Second, states and institutions may use these programs to obtain additional support from alumni, business, and industry. The programs may be incentives to enhance areas of strength. Since funding is beyond the equity levels generated by formulas or other mechanisms, institutions may have more flexibility in directing these funds to specific disciplines. Such programs are also attractive to the funding source. States can allocate surpluses and other nonrecurring funds for endowments, and institutions could allocate year-end savings and surplus fund balances to these programs. Implementation of endowment programs at the institutional level could serve as an incentive for academic departments to use funds more effectively.

Reallocation. Reallocation tends to be related to funding level. Beginning in the mid-1970s, reallocation became synonomous with cutback, and most states and publicly supported institutions were confronted with mid-year recisions and reductions attributable to the economic recession. In general, higher education judged the cutbacks to be temporary and used short-term strategies of reductions in nonpersonnel areas, including equipment, physical plant, and travel. The recession was not short term, and the results of the cutback strategies are more significant than intended. The large deficiencies in instructional equipment are caused, to some degree, by these short-term cutback strategies.

However, 1984 was a year of change in the financial milieu. Voters rejected tax cutting and limiting proposals in some states, and, in others, tax increases to fund educational reform were enacted. Public willingness to pay for better schools and colleges is clearly evident. Perhaps the memory of past years of economic downturn influenced many governors to target some portion of higher education funding to research and high technology centers to attract business and industry with the purpose of aiding economic development and perhaps averting future economic crises. From an overall funding perspective, a predominant financing trend for the 1980s is increased state financial support, although the support may be targeted to new programs.

Nonetheless, states should consider reallocation approaches. One alternative available to most states is to shift resources from the capital budget to instructional operations. Many states issued massive bond issues in the 1960s for the rapid expansion of higher education facilities, and many of these issues will soon be retired. Also, in most states new bonds are issued each year for additional expansion even though such construction may not be fully justified based on demographics or other quantitative factors. By placing a moratorium on new construction, states could free up resources that could be dedicated to instructional improvement and thereby reallocate funds within the higher education system. Or, as was recently implemented in New Jersey, states could raise funds through a bond issue to finance new operating programs, to purchase equipment, or to establish permanent endowments for instructional programs. For states with significant deferred capital maintenance requirements, it may be in the public interest to establish and fund these programs with the available resources.

At the institutional level, the current environment provides ample opportunities to reallocate from ancillary functions to instruction and to establish allocation procedures within instruction. The renewed emphasis on teaching and learning reflects a climate in which noninstructional activities may be scrutinized more carefully. Institutions with non-self-supporting athletic and public service programs should evaluate both the resource allocation level and the effectiveness of such programs to determine if funding levels are warranted. Also, institutions should review allocation of resources within those academic departments that are in decline. If the decision is made to maintain stable departmental funding, then faculty and administrators should determine how to reallocate resources to improve instruction. When education enrollments declined precipitously and educational departmental funding remained stable, many institutions missed an opportunity to focus available resources on improved school/college partnerships and other important goals.

Summary

As a result of the current emphasis on instructional quality, higher education has increased opportunities to change state and institutional budgeting systems to promote student learning and development. The financial environment is such that additional resources are available to make significant improvements. If budget policy emphasizes improvement of learning, the goal of institutional excellence is more likely to be attained. Prototypes are available for states and institutions seriously considering qualitative changes to the funding process. Multi-year funding contracts can ameliorate the uncertainty and anxiety that accompany funding reductions associated with enrollment decline and simultaneously provide a reasonable time frame for implementation and measurement of qualitative improvements. Such approaches are also necessary for responding to new accountability requirements. By providing seed money and cost recoveries for teaching, states and institutions demonstrate that instructional activities have equal or greater rewards than research. By adopting frontloading strategies that emphasize comprehensive remedial education and advising programs institutions can better retain students and provide more effective access.

While the public appears willing to support excellence in education at any cost, other methods of finance are available and should be considered. Charging students fees dedicated to instructional improvements is a practical and politically saleable approach to providing the funding margin of difference. By establishing permanent endowments, states and institutions can provide more stable funding, emphasize scholarly activity, and use nonrecurring funds. States should also consider shifting resources from construction of new facilities to instructional improvement or dedicating funds no longer necessary to retire indebtedness on higher education facilities to instructional improvement.

At the institutional level, the renewed emphasis on teaching and learning provides greater opportunities to reallocate from ancillary functions. Further, judicious planning and allocation of human resources to instructional improvement activities is critical.

The budget communicates values and priorities and, when policies are appropriately structured, even minimal financial incentives can produce impressive results. The fiscal risk of many of the proposed changes for instructional improvement is small and limited, particularly when compared to potential returns.

References

Association of American Colleges (AAC). *Integrity in the College Curriculum: A Report to the Academic Community.* Washington, D.C.: Association of American Colleges, 1985.

Bennet, W. J. *To Reclaim a Legacy.* Washington, D.C.: National Endowment for the Humanities, 1984.

Folger, J. K. "Assessment of Quality for Accountability." In J. K. Folger (ed.), *Financial Incentives for Academic Quality.* New Directions for Higher Education, no. 48. San Francisco, Calif.: Jossey-Bass, 1984.

National Institute of Education (NIE). *Involvement in Learning: Realizing the Potential of American Higher Education.* Washington, D.C.: National Institute of Education, 1984.

Brenda N. Albright is associate director for finance at the Tennessee Higher Education Commission.

A faculty allocation formula can be developed that is both internally acceptable and externally justifiable.

Allocating Faculty in the Budgeting Process

Gene A. Kemper

During the past decade, many institutions of higher education have encountered substantially increased need to retain public confidence in their integrity. This has caused thoughtful institutions to review their policies and practices to ensure internally acceptable and externally justifiable performance. These institutions have frequently initiated, or at least revitalized, long-range strategic planning activities. Such activities have been coupled with efforts to find procedures to measure the quality of institutional performance and to justify the resources required to address the long-range plan. As part of these efforts, the University of North Dakota (UND) conducted a feasibility study to develop a faculty funding formula that would serve as an internally acceptable guideline and an externally justifiable procedure for allocating faculty in the budgeting process.

Need for the Study

Since 1966, the university has engaged in the three long-range planning activities. The final study, a three-year effort, resulted in a ten-year plan issued in 1980. This document served as the basis for a program evaluation effort that reviewed each degree program offered by the university to determine how the program supported

D. J. Berg, Gerald M. Skogley (Eds.). *Making the Budget Process Work.* New Directions for Higher Education, no. 52. San Francisco: Jossey-Bass, December 1985.

the long-range plan. The evaluation recommendations, issued in 1981, completed an extensive five-year planning effort.

During the period of these studies, 1966 to 1981, headcount enrollment increased from 6.4 thousand to 10.8 thousand and has since tentatively stabilized at slightly over 11 thousand. However, state appropriations have not been sufficient to fully fund the full-time equivalent faculty positions generated by a funding formula previously used by the State Board of Higher Education (SBHE) and funded by the legislature. It became abundantly evident to university administrators that substantial effort would be required to return to full formula funding. Furthermore, it seemed an opportune time to review the current formula and suggest appropriate formula revisions.

The Current (1981) Formula. Three of the state's then eight institutions of higher education are on faculty formula budgeting. State funded salary dollars are based on the number and kind of students who are expected to enroll during an upcoming biennium. The term *full-time equivalent* (FTE) is used to refer to both faculty and student numbers. The basis for the formula is the student credit hour. The first step in the formula, as it applies at UND, involves projecting the student credit hours (SCH) generated at four different levels during each year of the biennium. These levels are lower division (freshman and sophomore courses), upper division (junior and senior courses), upper division engineering courses, and graduate courses. Once estimated, the credits are converted to FTE students (FTES). This is done by dividing the projected semester credits for each year by thirty-two for the undergraduate SCH and by twenty-four for the graduate SCH.

The resulting FTES are converted to FTE faculty (FTEF) by using another set of divisors. For the lower division level, twenty-five FTES generate one FTEF, for the upper division level, seventeen FTES generate one FTEF, and for the upper division engineering and graduate levels, twelve FTES generate one FTEF. The total of the FTEF is the instructional faculty.

Administrative faculty positions are determined by allocating one-half FTEF for each ten FTE instructional faculty positions up to fifty, and another one-half FTEF for each thirty FTE instructional faculty over fifty. Extracurricular faculty positions are determined by allocating five FTEF for the first 500 FTES and an additional one FTEF for each succeeding 500 FTES.

The institutional total FTEF allocation is the summation of the instructional faculty, administrative faculty, and extracurricular faculty. This total FTEF is multiplied by a university average salary determined by the State Board of Higher Education yielding the sum of money to be used for faculty salaries.

The Purpose and Approach of the Study

Although the then current formula was simple to apply, it does have obvious shortcomings. The university activity to develop an alternative formula was called the Foundation Funding Study with stated purpose to develop a method for determining faculty funding that would more appropriately and distinctly reflect the following factors: (1) the departmental needs for specialized faculty to offer the currently approved discipline programs; (2) suitable ratios of student credit hour to full-time equivalent faculty incorporating, for example, constraints imposed by accreditation standards; (3) adequate time for scholarly and service activites; and (4) salary levels sensitive to a market value concept.

Although the study focused primarily on faculty funding it also included data regarding the need for research/service assistants, secretarial/clerical staff, and other support staff. (These data are not discussed here.)

Higher education experience throughout the nation seems to indicate a formula method for determining faculty resources is more acceptable as a means of providing funding equity among institutions of a statewide system than it is as a means of determining funding allocations within an individual institution. A legitimate criticism of most formulas, including those discussed here, is that all critical factors that determine faculty resource needs are not identifiably included, or even considered, in the formula. Recognizing that a university is a complex organization and a perfect formula is possibly not attainable, the UND approach sought the development of a formula that would be externally justifiable for acquisition of funding and internally acceptable as a flexible guideline for allocation of resources.

The most important aspect of the study approach, from the point of internal acceptability, was that academic departments had direct input of teaching load data that was used to develop the initial version of an alternative formula. Similar studies at other institutions developed somewhat comparable formulae using averages of data obtained from peer institutions. The only peer institution teaching load data used in the study was to validate the proposed formula.

The particular approach was chosen to directly address the stated purpose. The study essentially had two components. The first component was an assessment of the number of faculty required to offer the currently authorized programs to students with majors, minors, concentrations, and so forth, in that discipline. This assessment was based on curricular offerings, not on enrollment, and addressed factor one (see above). The second component, being identification of suitable student credit hour to faculty ratios, was enrollment driven and addressed factor two. Each of these components determined the number of faculty required to support the departmental teaching responsibilities. These two estimates were then adjusted to reflect the departmental research and service activities, again from data initially recommended by the department. Presumably, an acceptable estimate of an appropriate departmental staffing level would be the larger of these adjusted estimates.

The Process. In order to meet potential implementation timelines, the study had a short time for completion. The study document was designed to require minimal information from the departments. To keep the study in motion, a committee of four representatives of the offices of academic affairs and of business and finance was formed with the office of academic affairs responsible for coordinating the effort. This committee initiated the study process in September 1981. By early November, the committee had met with the dean of each involved college, developed an approach, and drafted a study document that was reviewed by the president, vice-presidents for academic affairs and for business and finance, and the council of deans. At that time, the document was sent to the academic departments to be completed and returned to the office of academic affairs by January 1, 1982. Prior to the return date, committee members, upon invitation, visited individually with chairpersons, and visited with entire departments. By late January, the committee issued a preliminary analysis of the data that was reviewed by the president and vice-presidents and sent to the deans. The deans reviewed the preliminary analysis with their departments after which a committee representative met with each dean to negotiate appropriate modifications of the findings. The resulting data was analyzed and returned to the deans for final review. The final report on the faculty funding study, excluding the analysis of the support personnel data, was issued on March 31, 1982.

Perhaps the most illustrative way to describe the study is to examine the data collection document sent to each academic department. This document, with minor revisions for clarity, is shown below. A cover memo was sent to each chairperson with the document. The memo was to clearly state the purpose of the study, stipulate that it was a feasibility study, indicate that the requested data was not available elsewhere on campus, and assure the chairperson that the department and dean would have opportunity to review the recommendations for possible negotiated modifications prior to preparation of the final study report.

Foundation Funding Study Document The information requested from your department will be used to determine two distinct levels of full-time equivalent faculty (FTEF) required to support your class offerings. One such level will specify the number of FTEF your department suggests is required to support all classes now offered by your department. This number of FTEF is related to the number of student credit hours (SCH) generated per semester by your department and will be called the TOTAL FTEF.

The other level will specify the number of FTEF your department suggests is required to offer courses in your department that are required of students "in your discipline." Students "in your discipline" include undergraduate *and* graduate

1. students majoring or minoring in your discipline,

2. students with a teaching major or minor in your discipline, and

3. students with related fields concentration majors or minors with concentration courses in your department.

Courses required of students "in your discipline" include electives in your department normally taken by these students to complete the credit hour requirements for their major or minor. The courses collectively required by these students are referred to as your CORE CURRICULUM. The concept of a CORE CURRICULUM is to identify those courses in your department that need to be offered to make your program available to students "in your discipline" and as such is not related to the actual headcount of students served by your department, the number of majors and minors nor to the number of SCH generated by your department. The corresponding number of required FTEF will be called the CORE FTEF.

Please note that for a course not to be listed in the CORE CURRICULUM is an indication of the relevance of the course to students "in your discipline" and is not a reflection on the quality or importance of the course. Indeed, it is probable that service oriented courses might not be in the CORE CURRICULUM. However, the student credit hour load for such courses will be accounted for in the determination of the TOTAL FTEF.

A stated purpose of Foundation Funding is to acknowledge the departmental needs for specialized faculty and thus provide a "critical mass" of faculty to viably offer the CORE CURRICULUM. The university recognizes that specialized courses in your department require faculty with corresponding specializations. Some of those specializations can be expected to be compatible in the sense that often one faculty member will be capable of teaching and/or directing research in two or more related areas. On the other hand, some specialties are not in this sense compatible and will require individual faculty to teach and/or direct research in these areas. Naturally, several of your courses might be such that any professional in your discipline can indeed effectively teach these courses. However, your faculty specialization requirements imply that the number of faculty needed to offer your departmental programs cannot be obtained, for example, simply by dividing the number of semester hours to be offered in a given semester by some given faculty teaching load.

Two forms have been developed to facilitate the identification of the CORE CURRICULUM and the corresponding personnel resources. These forms are called the CORE CURRICULUM COURSE SHEET and the FOUNDATION FUNDING PERSONNEL DATA SHEET. The COURSE SHEET is categorized according to the level of courses (LOWER DIVISION, 100-200 level; UPPER DIVISION, 300-400 level; GRADUATE, 500 level). The information on the DATA SHEET will be used to determine the number of FTEF needed to viably offer the CORE CURRICULUM, that is, it will be used to determine the "critical mass" faculty called the CORE FTEF. In addition to the DATA SHEET, information will be used to determine the FTEF desired to support your current and projected class offerings (based on SCH generated), that is, the TOTAL FTEF. These determinations will be performed by the office of academic affairs and recorded on the DATA SHEET with a copy returned to your department for review.

Figure 1. Core Curriculum Course Sheet

Department/Area

Lower Division Courses

Course Number	SS	Sem Hrs Credit	Desirable Class Size	Course Name
. . .	. . .	. . .	. . .	. . .

Note: There were similar sheets for upper division courses and graduate level courses.

Figure 2. Foundation Funding Personnel Data Sheet

		Course Level		
		Lower Div. 100-200	Upper Div. 300-400	Grad. 500
1.	Department/Area:			
2.	Total number of semester hour credits from CORE CURRICULUM offered during average semester.			
3.	Number of full time equivalent <u>teaching</u> faculty (FTETF) required to teach courses corresponding to (2).			
4.	Desirable SCH/FTEF ratio.			
5.	Amount (%) of time a full time faculty member should be provided for unsponsored research.			
6.	Amount (%) of time a full time faculty member should be provided for service activities.			
7.	Number of FTETF required to teach summer CORE CURRICULUM courses during average Summer Session.			

8. Amount (%) of FTEF time required for chairing department
    at: CORE FTETF staffing level ____%,
         TOTAL FTEF staffing level ____%

9. Number of Graduate Research Assistants (GRA) and Graduate
    Service Assistants (GSA) required to support the depart-
    mental activities at: CORE FTETF staffing level ____GRA,
                                                     ____GSA
                           TOTAL FTEF staffing level ____GRA
                                                     ____GSA

10. Number and classification (Secretary I, II, III, IV, Clerk
    I, II, and so forth) of persons required to support the
    departmental activities at:

    CORE FTETF staffing level   TOTAL FTEF staffing level

    Number   Classification   Number   Classification
    _____   _____   _____   _____
    _____   _____   _____   _____
    _____   _____   _____   _____

11. If you wish please attach other personnel requirements
    necessary to support the departmental activities at the
    CORE FTETF level and/or the TOTAL FTEF level. Include
    an explanation of the need for these personnel.

12. Signatures:

    _____   _____   _____   _____
    Department/Area Chair   Date   Dean   Date

13. These determinations will be performed by the office of
    academic affairs and recorded on the DATA SHEET with a
    copy returned to your department for your review.

    CORE FTEF _____   SUMMER CORE FTEF _____

    TOTAL FTEF _____   SUMMER TOTAL FTEF _____

COURSE SHEET (Figure 1) Instructions

Please complete the CORE CURRICULUM COURSE SHEETS corresponding to those categories appropriate to your department. For a description of the column labeled "SS," refer to Item 7 in the following section.

DATA SHEET (Figure 2) Instructions

The items on the DATA SHEET will be discussed individually in numerical order.

Item 1: Please supply the name of your department/area.

Item 2: The requested information is the average number of semester hour credits of CORE CURRICULUM courses that would need to be offered each semester in order for a student "in your discipline" to complete the program in a normal time period (for example, four years for an undergraduate degree). In essence, you are requested to examine your CORE CURRICULUM and determine which courses need to be offered and how often, much as you now do when building your time schedule of classes. Courses not offered every semester and variable credit hour courses shoud be averaged into this determination. Please recall these course offerings are not to include multiple sections. Additionally, summer session activities are not to be included in departmental responses to Item 2.

This information is requested for the three categorizations of CORE CURRICULUM courses as indicated on the DATA SHEET and as described on the COURSE SHEETS.

Item 3: Note the concept of a full-time equivalent TEACHING faculty (FTETF). A FTETF is a faculty member with only teaching and related activities. That is, a person without research or service activities. The research/service activity is accounted for in Items 5 and 6. Teaching and related activities are to be interpreted as indicated on the Faculty Activity Record Form, that is, direct instruction, coaching, supervision, course development/improvement, professional reading, and so forth.

As a point of reference, if in your department a FTETF would be expected to teach fifteen semester hour credits and a FTEF spends 40 percent of time on research/service and 60 percent of time on teaching, then the teaching load of a FTEF would be 60 percent of fifteen hours or nine hours.

For each of the three CORE CURRICULUM categorizations, you are requested to provide the number of FTETF required to teach the CORE CURRICULUM semester hour credits as indicated in Item 2. In determining this information, please pay particular attention to the individual specialties represented in your departmental programs.

Item 4: With due regard for reasonableness and reality, you are requested to indicate a desirable student credit hour per full-time equivalent faculty ratio (SCH/FTEF) for lower division, upper division and graduate level courses. Please note the use of FTEF rather than FTETF as indicated in Item 3. Departments having special concerns (accreditation constraints, individual instruction, and so forth) are expected to provide substantiation for "low" ratios. (Please attach to DATA SHEET.)

Items 5 and 6: Please indicate, again with due regard for reasonableness and reality, the percent of a FTEF effort that could be expected to be devoted to research/creative or scholarly activity and to professional service (for example, departmental/college/university committee work, governance, advising/counseling students, and so forth, but not including chairperson responsibilities). These numbers facilitate the conversion of FTETF to FTEF.

Item 7: This item addresses summer session activity. If your department serves students "in your discipline" who attend the university primarily during the summer (for example, teachers) or who have summer commitments as part of their degree curriculum (for example, internship and practicum activities) then it is expected that some of your CORE CURRICULUM courses need to be offered in the summer session. Please indicate these courses on the COURSE SHEETS simply b placing a mark (X) in the column having the heading "SS". Then indicate on the DATA SHEET the Full Time Equivalent TEACHING Faculty (FTETF) required to teach the number of semester hour credits from the summer CORE CURRICULUM offered during an average Summer Session. (As in Item 2, CORE CURRICULUM course offerings are not to include multiple sections.) This number will be converted to FTEF by the office of academic affairs, recorded in Item 13 on the DATA SHEET as SUMMER CORE FTEF and reported to your department.

For departments not described in the previous paragraph, the SUMMER CORE FTEF might be zero. This does not imply the nonexistence of departmental summer offerings. Indeed, the SUMMER TOTAL FTEF in Item 13 will be calculated using the ratios indicated in Item 4.

Item 8*: The number to be provided should represent the required effort as perceived by the chairperson.

Items 9, 10, 11*: These items reflect the required staff (including graduate research/service assistants) to support the CORE CURRICULUM and to support the current departmental offerings (that is, your current level of SCH per semester). Note GTAs are not included. GTA support is exchanged for FTEF support as it is now.

Item 12: Self-explanatory.

Item 13: Self-explanatory.

*In Items 8-11, the CORE FTETF is simply the sum of the entries on the DATA SHEET corresponding to Item 3. TOTAL FTEF staffing level is to be interpreted as your current FTEF level (that is, the FTEF level in your department for the first semester academic year 1981-1982).

There was an additional enclosure with the study document that provided an illustration of the calculations to be performed by the office of academic affairs. That illustration, according to the departments, provided considerable insight into the information that would be determined from the raw data provided by the department.

An examination of the data sheet reveals a substantial similarity between the current formula and the enrollment-driven component of the proposed formula. Indeed, courses are still categorized as lower division, upper division, and graduate level, SCH/FTEF ratios are used (Item 4) and administrative faculty are included (Item 8). However, these factors are now applied at the departmental rather than institutional level. Additionally, there is an identifiable inclusion for research (Item 5), service (Item 6) and special needs (Items 9 and 11). The similarity provides certain advantages. For example, the general concept is familiar because of the current formula and data collected by institutional research efforts for the current formula could be applied to the proposed formula and used to estimate desirable SCH/FTEF ratios (Item 4). Finally, discussions that occurred during the developmental process and suggested appropriate modifications to the current formula would provide a suitable enrollment drive component.

The curriculum-driven component, that is the CORE FTEF, is also a familiar concept on campus. This is due to state-system policy that institutions within the system that do not generate sufficient formula faculty are provided a number of faculty sufficient to offer their approved curriculum. This minimum staffing policy is similar to the concept of a departmental CORE FTEF. The CORE CURRICULUM COURSE SHEET was utilized to encourage the departments to carefully consider their CORE COURSES and the sequence and frequency of these courses. The data then becomes a base for determining the departmental minimum staffing or CORE FTEF.

Inclusion of the CORE FTEF determination in the study served more than to address factor one of the formula. During the period the study was conducted, the institution, according to a system-wide consultant's study, was to begin to experience a substantial enrollment decline. This projected decline contributed to the institution's sensitivity regarding the possibility of losing faculty, as determined by the formula, to the point where the then currently approved curriculum could not be offered. It was therefore a strength of the study to include this component.

Analysis and Validation. The proposed new formula determinations are easily inferred from the PERSONNEL DATA SHEET. Item 3 provides the academic year core teaching faculty for each course level. These numbers when adjusted by Items 5 and 6 produce the core teaching/research/service faculty. Finally, special adjustments using Items 8 and 11 produce the TOTAL FTEF. Similar computations apply to the summer session data.

Once these calculations have been completed, the results can be used with other easily obtainable data to produce considerable information at the departmental, college, and institutional levels. For example, using the projected SCH at each level, current SBHE formula, and the proposed formula, it is easy to calculate the FTEF determined by the current SBHE formula and the FTEF determined by the proposed formula. These calculated allocations can then be compared with the actual FTEF allocation. Such comparisons reveal the perceived degree of relative wellness between departments or colleges within the university. By careful comparison of peer institution teaching load data the wellness of the university was judged.

There was another reason to use peer institution data. By comparing the departmental TOTAL FTEF with the FTEF obtained by using departmental averages from a group of peer institutions, in this case the Southern University Group (SUG) (Office of Institutional Research, 1980), the validity of the enrollment-driven component of the study was substantiated. The study was further validated by noting that UND's undergraduate tuition and required fees were the median when ranked with comparable data of the SUG institutions.

The analyses and comparisons were made at the departmental, college, and university levels. The university level summary reported that for academic year 1981—82 the State Board of Higher Education formula specified 419 FTEF, the curriculum-based teaching/research/service faculty numbered 543 FTEF. Using the Southern University Group average teaching load, the FTEF numbered 548. The SUG comparison suggests the departmental recommended SCH/FTEF ratios provide a reasonable first estimate for later fine tuning should the proposed approach be adopted. However, when the larger of the CORE FTEF and the TOTAL FTEF for each department was used as the Foundation Funding Study recommended staffing level, the resulting FTEF numbered 585. It is evident that considerable effort would be needed to fine tune the data in this recommendation. A close examination of that data at the departmental level reveals there are, fortunately, few departments principally in two of the six involved colleges that would need to rethink their CORE FTETF recommendation. There is, therefore, reason to expect that the feasibility study produced a formula that, with appropriate adjustments, would address the first three stated factors.

The fourth stated factor, that of salary levels sensitive to a market value concept, yielded an unexpected result during the analysis. The study committee proposed to use national average salary data in each discipline from an Oklahoma State University (OSU) study (Office of Institutional Research, 1982) rather than a single university average salary as used by the SBHE. Unexpectedly, the funding level determined by using the university average salary method was essentially the same as the funding level when the national average salary by discipline was used. The same agreement did not hold at the departmental level. Thus, there appeared to be reason to examine the funding mechanism used by the office of academic affairs to allocate funds to the colleges.

The Study's Influence

The Foundation Funding Study analyses and recommendations were discussed with the council of deans and at the annual chairpersons workshop. External to the campus, the study was discussed with the commissioner of higher education, his staff, and the governor. Although the study recommendations as such have not been implemented, the study has indirectly been influential in two significant areas. The first evidence of this occurred when the state higher education system was invited to participate in a legislative funding study. The purpose of the study was to determine the adequacy and the appropriateness of current funding methods applied to postsecondary education and to develop a long-range plan for future funding of postsecondary education. One of the several task forces considered alternative faculty funding methods including the Foundation Funding Study. The task force recommendations, which were supported by the State Board of Higher Education, effected three slight, but significant, changes in the then current faculty funding formula. One of the changes included a method of enrollment buffering that averages enrollments over a three-year period. The other two changes were with regard to the conversion of SCH to FTEF. At the undergraduate level, a FTES was redefined to equate to thirty semester credits per academic year rather than thirty-two. At the graduate level the FTES/FTEF ratio was reduced from 12/1 to 9/1. These changes were to have been incorporated into the funding request of the state legislature. Unfortunately, the economic situation within the state had resulted in a salary freeze during the 1983–1985 biennium. As a result, the top priority funding request of the 1985 legislature was to appropriately restore salary levels. Although the new funding formula was not used during the 1985 legislative session, it is expected to remain an important part of the long-range plan for the funding of postsecondary education.

The salary appropriations to the university for 1985–1986 did include funding for a market value adjustment. Knowing the Foundation Funding Study analyses had revealed discrepancies between the departmental average salaries and comparative OSU national data, the office of academic affairs updated that comparison to determine the discrepancies based on the most current data. A similar comparison using the OSU Region I data was eventually used as the major factor in determining adjustments to the college base budgets for the forthcoming year. The market value adjustment thus provided a significant opportunity for application of the study.

The Foundation Funding Study has at times been a reference when departments were justifying the need for additional faculty positions or the need to retain a vacated position. There is definite potential for utilizing this study, or a refinement or derivative thereof UND, like other institutions, will increase its efforts to more effectively acquire resources, efficiently allocate new resources, and reallocate existing resources to maintain quality in existing educational opportunities and to develop new educational opportunities.

The university is now at the midpoint of the last ten-year plan. As the institution reexamines the long range goals and sharpens the goals for the next five years, it is simultaneously developing an undergraduate program review process to supplement the existing graduate level process. There is need for internally applicable, flexible guidelines for allocating faculty in the budgeting process in order to appropriately link budgeting, planning, and program review. Only then can the quest for continued academic excellence be achieved.

References

Office of Institutional Research. "1981–1982 Faculty Salary Survey of Institutions Belonging to the National Association of Universities and Land Grant Colleges (NASULGC)." Stillwater: Oklahoma State University, 1982.

Office of Institutional Research. "Southern University Group Teaching Load Data Exchange Fall 1980." Blackburg: Virginia Polytechnic Institute and State University, 1980.

Gene A. Kemper is the associate vice-president for academic affairs at the University of North Dakota and was chairman of the Foundation Funding Study Committee.

A decentralized administrative environment can be a means to ensure the effective allocation of resources through participative decision making.

Resource Allocation in a Decentralized Environment

John L. Green, Jr.
David G. Monical

There are probably as many different ways of allocating resources in institutions of higher education as there are presidents. In other words, each president has adopted an internal administrative style and method of resource allocation that is unique to that institution. This is due, in part, to the fact that institutions are funded through a variety of sources, administered through a variety of structures, and function in a variety of environmental settings.

The decisions related to the allocation of resources in a college or university are among the most important decisions made by administrators and governing boards in higher education. Administrators realize that the need for additional resources is unending, but, because resources are always limited, the matter of establishing priorities in the allocation process must be addressed.

Decisions made on the allocation of resources determine institutional direction during the upcoming year and in years to come. To make responsible decisions about resource allocation, a sound base of information should be available to the decision makers. The integration of the planning and budgeting processes provides the

D. J. Berg, Gerald M. Skogley (Eds.). *Making the Budget Process Work.* New Directions for Higher Education, no. 52. San Francisco: Jossey-Bass, December 1985.

necessary linkage among environmental factors and institutional priorities and resource allocation.

Strategic planning focuses attention on the major issues confronting the institution and on the effective deployment of institutional resources to address those issues. It involves the application of a total systems approach to management. With this approach, the decision-making parts of an organization's mechanism are coordinated; strategic planning formalizes channels for information flow between administration and faculty.

A more effective method of resource allocation in colleges and universities is needed. This can best be accomplished by implementing a system of strategic planning in an organizational environment that promulgates decentralization of administrative responsibilities.

This chapter describes a decentralized administrative structure implemented at one institution, how the structure helps integrate the planning and budgeting process, and the effectiveness of the resulting resource allocations. This case study approach may provide suggestions for organizational structures and strategies at other similar institutions.

Strategic Planning

The current form of strategic planning emanated from the annual budget processes of the 1950s. Annual budgets were prepared for each function and budgetary unit (division or department) of an institution. These one-year budgets represented an annual plan of operation. The budgets included the revenue forecasts, operating expenditures, and capital requirements of the institution. During the 1950s, institutional structures were relatively simple, academic offerings were not overly extensive, and the economy was fairly stable, and the budgetary system matched the business climate—conservative and not overly aggressive. Long-range planning had not become a formalized process, except perhaps for capital items.

But times changed. Multi-campus systems evolved, enrollment grew rapidly, technological developments surged, and the rate of change accelerated, making the future more uncertain and requiring more effective preparation of operating budgets and capital expenditure plans. Management by objectives (MBO) became the essential tool of effective administrators in the 1960s. Forecasting also was introduced during this era, with three- to five-year forecasts being made of enrollments, revenues, expenditures, and environmental factors.

This was the beginning of formalized planning. Emphasis began to shift from the "numbers game" to the future direction of the institution—what it should be as compared to the way it was. Strategists were sought and alternative strategic directions for an institution were examined. Competition intensified and it soon became evident that successful institutions had developed a vision of the future as well as a strategic approach for realizing that vision.

New methods of planning were developed that dealt with environmental factors. Strategies that would ensure greater success were implemented as were administrative plans of action to implement these strategies. Resources were allocated on the basis of creating an academic advantage, and systems of monitoring progress were established to help ensure success. Strategic planning, strategic thinking, and strategic management were born.

Strategic planning poses four fundamental questions: Where have we been and where are we now? Where will we be in the future by following our present course? Where do we want to be? How will we get there? The successful performance of an organization relates directly to effective planning, decision making, and execution. An organization that determines where it plans to go, what it plans to do, and how it plans to do it can make better decisions, more effectively manage resources and operations, and adjust more readily to change.

Strategic planning provides a structural approach to planning, and thereby gives overall institutional direction by integrating individual departmental plans with the institution's plan. It also helps minimize the bureaucratic tendency to subordinate institutional welfare to that of a few departments. Another advantage of strategic planning is the simultaneous use of top-down, bottom-up, and team approaches to planning, thus enhancing the value of communication within the organization. Administrators and faculty gain a better understanding of how their aspirations and actions can support the objectives of the institution and the goals of departments. At the same time, the institution gains insight into the needs and desires of its faculty.

There are four phases of strategic planning: (1) environmental scanning and analysis, (2) institutional mission and objectives, (3) departmental goals and strategies, and (4) action plans and priorities.

The first phase, environmental scanning and analysis, includes an assessment of the organization's present situation, its past, and its forecasted future. Two major components of this phase are the internal and external environments. The internal environment is an objectively drawn self-portrait of the organization both retrospectively and prospectively. Two of the major components of the internal environment analysis include the preparation of profiles for each strategic planning unit, which help to identify strengths and weaknesses, and the forecasting of future states of performance of the planning units. Some institutions also develp a profile of management's beliefs, attitudes, and values and include these in the internal environment analysis. The external environment review, however, is tantamount to recognizing the external opportunities and threats that face the organizational components of the institution as well as the institution as a whole.

The second phase in strategic planning is the development or updating of the institutional objectives. The mission statement is essential to the preparation of the strategic plan because it provides the overall framework for the operation, development, and growth of the organization. The mission statement sets forth the purposes of the organization and what it is striving to be. Both tradition and social expectations influence the mission of an institution to a significant degree. The formulation of the mission statement is also influenced by the results of the first phase of planning (environmental scanning and analysis). The mission statement is broad in scope and addresses a long period, perhaps decades. However, the statement is not for all time—it must be periodically updated.

From the mission statement, a set of institutional objectives is derived. A statement of objectives identifies desired states or future conditions and, therefore, is a statement of intent. An objective normally covers a time frame of from two to five years. Statements of objectives spell out the administration's intentions to bridge the gap between the present nature of the institution and what it should be, as addressed in the mission statement.

The third phase of the strategic planning process involves setting goals and developing alternative strategies. In part, goals relate to objectives but also address critical items identified during the first phase of planning, such as strategic issues, departmental strengths and weaknesses, and key success factors. Goals are operational indicators and have specific purposes, such as directing the growth of an activity or achieving levels of performance. Strategies represent different ways of accomplishing objectives and achieving goals. After reviewing alternative strategies, it is important to determine a preferred strategy (or strategies) to achieve the particular goal or objective.

The fourth phase of the strategic planning process is the preparation of action plans and the setting of priorities for each action plan. Action plans relate to goal statements and preferred strategies and should be viewed as statements of specific intentional behavior or actions that, when accomplished, contribute to the achievement of a goal and related strategies. A noteworthy feature of action plans is that they fix responsibility for specific actions and identify the resources required to complete the action, thereby building into this stage of the planning process the accountability and costs for outcomes of specific actions.

Setting priorities is a difficult but necessary part of the planning process. Flexibility should prevail so priorities can be changed to meet the challenges of an ever-changing institutional environment.

The political problems experienced by institutions attempting to successfully implement strategic planning are often the result of the lack of acceptance of planning techniques by the people involved in the planning process. Those who control the planning process, preferably the president and the governing board, control the future of the organization. However, individuals have their own ideas about the planning process and vested interests, and the many special interest groups associated with an institution make it difficult to design and implement a strategic planning system without recognizing the political forces at work.

Cooperation in the planning process is essential to its success. If each division and department goes its own way, there will never be an integrated strategic plan. Instead, a fragmented and self-serving arrangement of proposed activities will emerge that will not represent the plans that are in the best interests of the organization. The president should be aware that politics can sabotage the planning effort and should take appropriate steps at the outset to minimize and contain such political activity. This can be done, in part, by having the members of the organization who are involved in the planning process participate in a training program designed to familiarize them with the overall planning process.

At the same time, the president must take care not to build expectations that strategic planning will produce immediate positive results. Strategic planning is not a panacea; it will not resolve problems immediately after implementation, nor will the implementation be easy to administer. This realization will increase the probability of success in implementing strategic planning.

Further, the implementation of strategic planning should be

viewed as the beginning of a firm commitment by all who are involved in the process to devote the extra time and energies needed to plan successfully. It is not a one-time action but a continuous process performed in annual cycles and coupled with year-round involvement by administrators. The time and effort initially required should decrease slightly as personnel who are involved in the formulation and implementation of the strategic plan develop a better understanding of the process and of their own roles.

A danger does exist that the personnel involved in the planning process may become complacent about their planning responsibilities. If this happens, planning will tend to be viewed as a routine and informal exercise. Formalized planning is, therefore, at the very root of the philosophy of strategic planning, as distinguished from the so-called informal planning that characterizes the forecasting and piecemeal planning efforts at some institutions.

It is important not to rush into a full-blown planning process at the very beginning. The planning process and techniques should be built around the most important activities of the organization and allowed to evolve based on the organization's particular needs. Proper selection of the information, techniques, and process is particularly important in the early stages of the planning process to optimize planning effort and impact.

As strange as it may seem, formal planning is one of the most unnatural activities that takes place in an institution. Results-oriented administrators believe that action speaks louder than words. They often see formal planning as time taken away from teaching, research, and public service. Planning requires administrators to think differently and to redirect their attention and interests to the well-being of the institution for the next decade.

The president must be convinced that planning will improve the institution's performance and create a more competitive edge (academic excellence) for the academic areas within the institution. The president's involvement is crucial to initiating change in the organization; the president must motivate the administrators to plan in a formal way. When the president is convinced, then the planning actions of the president will speak louder than words.

One misconception of some presidents is the belief that they do not have to be directly involved in comprehensive planning. They regard planning as something to be delegated to subordinates without the active participation of the president. Although strategic planning does not guarantee success, institutions that use strategic planning generally outperform those that do not. While it is rare for a president to be formally trained to be a technical expert in planning, it is nonetheless essential that the president, as the chief executive officer of the institution, be committed to planning and accept the role of chief planner.

One of the most arduous and yet most fundamental tasks of an administrator is decision making. Strategic planning provides a framework for better decision making by enabling management to evaluate the potential consequences of alternative courses of action. Too often administrators make decisions without adequate analysis of their possible impact on the future of the institution. The change agents in the environment are never dormant. By reacting to change rather than being proactive, they can create a type of management that is unbearable to faculty and staff and can result in a loss of institutional viability.

A tradition of incremental institutional budgeting has hampered the implementation of a formalized planning process. While in some institutions departments have traditionally been allowed to individually plan and administer their own operations, this may not serve the best interests of the institution. In such cases, the president is limited in performing the role of chief planner of the total organization. Planning should be performed on an integrated basis, rather than independently or piecemeal. While decentralization of major academic areas is important, complete autonomy, independence, and lack of integration within the institutional planning structure are not recommended.

Decentralization

The decision to form a decentralized organization depends greatly on the style of administration a president possesses and supports. There are examples of highly effective organizations that favor a centralized structure, but today an increasing number of decentralized organizations in the United States are highly successful. Successful organizations are placing administrative emphasis on doing the right things, as opposed to the common belief that emphasis should be placed on doing things right.

A large number of organizations have developed the administrative skills to do things right (that is, to follow rules and regulations properly), but few organizations have learned how to do the right things (that is, those things that give the organization a competitive edge or make it excel in quality). In many colleges and universities, the administration concentrates its largest efforts on doing things right, with the result that a large bureaucracy created to ensure that a voluminous list of rules and regulations is followed. This type of administrative focus often overshadows more productive efforts to do the right things. For example, rules, regulations, policies, and procedures may prohibit faculty from experimenting with new programs. Bureaucratic structures in organizations can stifle the efforts of program heads to be creative and innovative and to seize opportunities that could make the institution excel.

Doing the right thing is directly related to strategic planning to achieve goals and requires good judgment and experience, the ability to take risks, and the willingness to be accountable for decisions. A recurring theme in strategic planning literature is that if the overall strategy of an organization is correct, any number of tactical errors can be made without significantly hurting the organization. However, if the overall strategy is wrong, the organization will fail in its efforts no matter how many tactical efforts are right.

Decentralization minimizes bureaucracy in an organization. Successful decentralization depends heavily on having effective administrators head the various operating units and also on participative management. Academic deans play key roles in a decentralized organization in higher education. They are the planners, the strategists, and the implementers of action and they are highly accountable for their actions.

Communication is another important factor that enables a decentralized institution to operate effectively. The administrative team must communicate and work together in a harmonious manner. Successful administrators usually have obtained a high level of skill in communicating with other administrative team members and support the concept of participative management in strategic planning.

Decentralization promotes a horizontal organizational structure rather than a pyramid type structure. The administration is a team that makes certain the right things are done. Although policies, procedures, rules, and regulations have a proper place in a decentralized environment, the emphasis does not rest on doing things right, but rather on doing the right things. Administrators who function successfully in a decentralized environment already know how to do things right. Their focus, interests, and concerns are all directed toward doing the right things.

Case Study

An actual instance of improved resource allocation in a decentralized environment involved the experience of Washburn University in Topeka, Kansas. Washburn is a public urban university with a municipal charter. This means it is neither a state chartered nor a privately chartered institution. Municipally chartered universities were plentiful in the 1950s, but only a few remain today; the others have become state chartered universities. Table 1 provides some vital statistics about Washburn University.

Washburn has characteristics of a private institution: a single governing board with a great deal of autonomy, relatively high tuition, a tuition-driven budget. Endowment and fundraising are key success factors. It also has characteristics of a state university: a governor appoints several members of the board of regents, state statutes pertain to operating policies, state appropriation is received, and legislative lobbying is a key factor for institutional success.

Contrary to national trends, Washburn has experienced increases in student enrollment each year over the past ten years, due, in part, to the fact that many students need to work part-time while they attend college and because an urban setting such as Washburn's provides more opportunity for employment and also for flexibility in scheduling classes.

The organizational structure at Washburn has been decentralized for four years. Academic deans report directly to the president. Previously, these deans reported to a vice-president for academic affairs. The academic deans have responsibility for their respective areas of academic programs. They are decision makers as opposed to paper shufflers and they are held accountable for doing the right things.

The Planning and Budgeting Committee. The five academic deans, along with four vice-presidents (administration, student affairs, academic affairs, and planning), and two directors (athletics and public television), constitute the executive management team of Washburn and serve, under the direction of the vice-president for planning, as the University's planning and budgeting committee. This committee was created to provide a mechanism to determine the University's overall budgetary needs and to reach consensus about the University's budget priorities for the up-coming fiscal year. In addition, because these priorities cannot effectively be established only in the context of a single fiscal year, the committee also serves as the central planning committee for the University.

Table 1. Vital Statistics About Washburn University

Background

- Founded by the Congregational Church in 1865 as Lincoln College.
- Changed its name to Washburn College in 1868 in remembrance of benefactor, Deacon Ichabod Washburn.
- Remained as a private college until 1940, when it received a municipal charter.

Governance

- Board of Regents, nine members. Three appointed by the Governor, four appointed by the City Council, the Mayor of Topeka is a member, and the remaining member is selected from among the State Board of Regents who govern the state chartered universities.
- There are 86 state statutes pertaining to the operation of Washburn University.

Funding

- State aid amounting to about 15.4 percent of the budget is one source of funding.
- City mill levy provides about 17.1 percent of the funding.
- County out-district tuition is 2.3 percent of the budget.
- Tuition and fees is 29.6 percent of the budget.
- Auxiliary enterprises is 9.3 percent of the budget.
- Restricted funds account for 14.1 percent of the funding.
- The remainder is miscellaneous revenue amounting to 10.1 percent.

Population

- Size of city is 150,000 people.
- Student enrollments are slightly over 7,000.

Academic Programs

- College of Arts and Sciences
- School of Law
- School of Business Administration
- School of Nursing
- School of Applied and Continuing Education

The creation of this central planning and budgeting committee, much broader in membership than other such committees at most universities, is based on a recognition of several factors crucial to achieving effective decision making within a university. The first factor is that, although the unit heads in a decentralized environment are primarily responsible for the successful operation of their own areas, many decisions require a broader understanding of the University as a whole. The determination of the future direction of the University should involve the largest possible constituency, including those who have the ultimate responsibility for the execution of the University's fundamental strategies. If the area heads participate in the allocation of the University's resources and in the determination of the University's direction, they will know why certain decisions were made and will be more likely to accept the consequences of those decisions than they would if they had not been part of the process. Thus, the committee serves as a mechanism to constantly reinforce a "sense of university" to complement the "importance of area" that already exists.

A second and related factor is that, for any of the University's strategies to succeed, it is necessary to have strong support and commitment from all of the operating units. Because a single course of action seldom presents itself and because all units of the institution are interrelated and interdependent, it is necessary to achieve the broadest possible consensus. Ultimately, most budgetary and planning decisions are judgmental, not simply matters of fact. In order to ensure that the right decision is made and that there is commitment to the successful execution of the strategy chosen, those involved with the execution are also involved with the decision making.

A third factor is that, within a decentralized administrative environment, a mechanism allowing for a broad dissemination of information relating to the university, its external environment, and each of its units is required. One of the most frequently encountered problems in an institution is a lack of understanding by the members of one area about the operations and activities of another area. Bringing together the heads of the operational units and forcing them to make decisions about the university as a whole forces them to learn about the operations of the other units. This requires that each of the area heads acquires a greater understanding of the interrelatedness of the components of the university and increases their understanding of the external factors that impinge on the institution. A central planning and budgeting committee provides the vehicle through which this information is transmitted, discussed, and analyzed.

The fourth factor is that a central planning committee pro-vides the appropriate mechanism for assessing accountability within a decentralized administrative structure. Once priorities are set and resources allocated, the units have broad latitude as to specific expen-ditures for their operations. Accountability occurs because the same group that determined the current year's allocations is responsible for assessing a unit's subsequent budgetary requests and evaluating the degree of success of the unit in achieving its goals. Because, as will be discussed below, the review of each unit's budget is not confined simply to an analysis of incremental increases but includes an overall review of all levels of operations, accountability is achieved because each unit is responsible to its peers for success or failure in attaining its goals.

Finally, a factor that led to the creation of a broad-based central planning and budgeting committee is the acknowlegment of the political environment that exists on all campuses. Each unit on a campus is constantly competing for resources with other campus units. The needs of the units are legitimate and always greater than the university's ability to satisfy. Many institutions attempt to eliminate the political influence on the decision-making process by having the fewest number of individuals make the broadest decisions involving the most resources. Thus, the typical hierarchical organ-izational structure eliminates participatory decision making at that level where the decisions affect the greatest number of individuals or units on the campus. In contrast, a decentralized structure, coupled with a central planning and budgeting committee, includes broad campus representation in making the university-wide deci-sions on resource allocation and budget priorities. Thus, each of the units is aware of why the decisions were made and participates in making the decisions.

The creation of a decentralized administrative structure is desirable for a variety of reasons, not the least of which is that those who are responsible for actions are invested with the authority for those actions. However, a mechanism is required to ensure that the right decisions are made and that the overall interests of the univer-sity are represented. A central planning and budgeting committee achieves this; it provides for an overall sense of the university, its decisions reflect a consensus of support, it improves the understand-ing of the university's units by its members, it provides for a process of accountability, and it recognizes the internal political environment of the campus. Thus, decentralization for the purpose of management is accompanied by participatory centralization for purposes of budgeting and planning.

The Planning and Budgeting Cycle. The planning and budgeting committee of Washburn University is a creation of and reports to the president. While the president does not meet with the committee at its regular meetings, he frequently suggests items for committee review and retains the right to modify any committee recommendation.

The committee's activities are ongoing over the entire fiscal year, with a focus on planning at certain times and on budget considerations at other times. During the fall semester the committee typically reviews actual cost data from previous years and budgeted cost data for the current year. In this period, base expenditures are reviewed and a determination is made of any reductions or realignments to be recommended by the committee. Any major changes in the base are agreed to by the committee, and subsequently reviewed by the president prior to the end of the fall semester. At the same time, the committee reviews current enrollments and revenues and reassesses estimates for the upcoming fiscal year. Basically, however, the fall semester can be viewed as the planning semester, where analysis of the previous year's activities is conducted, strategies are modified or adopted, and the major modifications to the university's strategic plan are considered.

The spring semester can be characterized as the budgeting semester. At this time, the unit budget requests are presented for consideration in light of the university's revised planning assumptions and its anticipated revenues for the upcoming fiscal year. The process begins with setting budgetary priorities and culminates with the committee's recommendations to the president in the late spring. These recommendations are then conveyed to the Board of Regents, who approve the development of the actual budget within the guidelines agreed to by themselves and the president. The final step is to adjust expenditures to match the best estimates of available resources. The actual budget itself is typically approved by the Board in May, with the new fiscal year commencing July 1.

During the summer session, the process is reassessed so that any procedural changes can be agreed upon by the beginning of the fall semester. In addition, this period affords an opportunity to compile information on the fiscal year just ended and to prepare a more detailed analysis on the budget of the new fiscal year. Because all members of the planning and budgeting committee are on twelve-month appointments, it is possible for the committee to continue to meet during the summer, although the frequency of meetings is reduced from that of the regular academic year.

The cycle itself tends to reinforce the participatory nature of the process. Major items of planning, policy, and the budget are considered and deliberated during periods when all the faculty are available for consultation. Because the formal budget and planning documents are not compiled until late in the spring, ample opportunity is available to reconsider earlier decisions in light of new information or changing circumstances. This flexibility is particularly important in institutions whose revenues are greatly dependent on external factors.

Full-Costing Information. One of the most important items that ensures the success of a decentralized organizational structure is information on costs and revenues of the university's operating units. This full-costing information provides basic data for the purpose of planning, setting budgetary priorities, and assessing the success of planning and budgeting strategies.

Full-costing involves the identification of the operational units of the institution that serve not only as expenditure centers but also as revenue generators. These are the cost centers, and all expenditures and revenues of the institution, both direct and indirect, are attributed to them. This allows for the determination of how well the cost centers covered their direct costs or total costs through generated revenues while also allowing for time-series analysis of changes in revenues and expenditures—both direct and indirect and on a per unit basis.

The importance of this type of information cannot be overstated for institutions whose budgets are primarily revenue-driven rather than expenditure-driven. Most frequently, this distinction corresponds to the distinction between independent and public institutions. In the case of institutions whose budgets are revenue-driven, expenditure levels are determined by the amounts of revenues available to the institution. Such revenues are typically closely aligned with enrollment levels. Thus, most independent colleges support between 60 and 75 percent of their current operating expenditures from tuition. In the case of Washburn, over 60 percent of revenues are driven by student credit hours as all state support is on a per credit hour basis. This situation is in contrast with most public institutions whose budgeting can be characterized as expenditure-driven, where a legislative body determines what will be an appropriate level of funding and provides the institution with resources. While enrollments may be a factor in determining the appropriate level of expenitures, enrollments typically are not a major factor in determining resource availability once the expeniture level has been decided on.

In institutions whose budgets are expenditure-driven the major budgeting questions center on how much the institution wishes to spend and how it gets that expenditure authority from its legislature. In contrast, institutions whose budgets are revenue-driven must determine how much revenue can realistically be generated and what level of expenditures those revenues will support. Because most educational costs are semi-fixed (they vary little in the short run), they do not tend to be directly affected by enrollment fluctuations; however, revenues are directly affected by student credit hour production in institutions whose budgets are revenue-driven. Because revenues are subject to sharp fluctuations due to enrollment changes while expenditures are not, revenue-driven institutions cannot afford to be inefficient in their expenditure patterns or to make mistakes in their allocations of resources. Hence, full-costing information is critical for planning and budgeting purposes in institutions whose budgets are revenue-driven.

In most organizations, a tendency toward budgetary incrementalism exists. However, institutions whose budgets are revenue-driven must constantly reevaluate programs and reassess base levels of program funding. Full-costing data provide the basic information for this evaluation and assessment by identifying which units are self-supporting and which units are subsidized. This type of information is not the end point but rather the beginning of the analysis of a unit's activity. Some units which are essential to fulfilling the institution's mission will always have full costs in excess of direct revenues and, thus, are subsidized. The appropriate planning and budgeting issue is the level of subsidy to provide to these units over time or in a given fiscal cycle. The full-costing information provides the impetus for raising a variety of questions about a unit's activities, its relationship to the institution's mission, the nature of its expenditure patterns, and the appropriate level of activity.

For example, some units will incur direct costs in excess of direct revenues regardless of the level of enrollment. If this is the case, care should be taken to ensure that enrollment increases are based on educational plans and that the effects of enrollment growth on the subsidy to the unit are recognized. Poor enrollment planning or a lack of understanding of the relationship among enrollments, revenues, and costs within the units can be potentially disastrous financially for institutions whose budgets are revenue-driven.

The importance of full-costing information in a decentralized environment cannot be overstated. It is the basic internal comparative information for planning and budgeting purposes. It provides the mechanism for assessment of a unit's achieving its stated financial goals as well as allowing for comparisons of financial standing among the units. Once the financial components of the units are understood, attention can then be focused on the significant issues of the institution's educational policies and mission.

A variety of full-costing models are available to institutions. It is important for institutions whose budgets are revenue-driven that such information be gathered, and used, in the planning and budgeting process. While full-costing information is important for any institution, it is crucial for an institution that chooses to operate with a decentralized administrative structure, since it provides the basic information to help make inter- and intra-unit comparisons and assessments.

In the case of Washburn University, full-costing information provides the members of the planning and budgeting committee with basic financial understanding of each other's units and enables the analysis of what programs will be maintained or created, for what reasons, and at what level of activity. It also helps make the budgetary priorities of the units explicit and subject to negotiation and agreement. It is hard to have a hidden agenda when full-costing data are shared with, and reviewed by, all of one's colleagues.

Summary. The implementation of a decentralized administrative structure at Washburn University has resulted in a number of improvements. Faculty and administrators are working together to set goals of excellence. This is done by reviewing the role and scope statements of each academic department of the University. Research activities have accelerated, and many of the departments and schools now have specific goals for research endeavors. Faculty and administrators are intimately involved in student enrollment forecasting and have become more actively involved in student recruitment. They have learned the necessity of dealing with the ever-changing environment and the importance of being innovative and competitive.

While these improvements are not always discretely measurable, the overall improvement of the University's status, academic quality, enrollment levels, and resource acquisitions (including gifts) is quite evident. In addition, the attitudes and behavior of the faculty and academic deans have become more positive and reflect an interest in the success of each department and school and of the University as a whole. Quality education is now recognized as essential to the success of the University. The setting of priorities within the academic units is understood as necessary to achieve the goal of excellence.

Since decentralization, the budget process has become integrated with the planning process so that funding decisions focus more on the support of institutional priorities than on the financing of specific objects of expenditure. The budget is now recognized as being the first year of the University's current strategic plan, which has resulted in more coherent decisions regarding the allocation of institutional resources.

Information, which once was gathered on an ad hoc basis, is now routinely generated for support of the planning and budgeting process. Full-costing information has become the initial focus for discussions regarding current and future resource allocations. Emphasis is given not only to incremental budget adjustments, but also to consideration of base levels of funding and operations consistent with institutional objectives and unit goals.

Resource allocation is subject to negotiated consensus, as opposed to fiat. The mere act of reaching consensus among such a diverse group as the planning and budgeting committee provides those acts with a legitimacy not always present in decisions made by smaller groups. The committee, in a decentralized structure, recognizes that there is more to budgeting and resource allocation than incrementalism and pro rata distribution. Participatory decision making acknowledges that budgeting and resource allocation are not matters of fact or formula, but of judgment as to the right thing to do.

The key to making any organizational process successful is people: They must be involved, committed, and accountable for their decisions. A decentralized administrative structure provides a process whereby the people who implement the resource allocation decisions participate in making the decisions.

John L. Green, Jr., is president of Washburn University and professor of management in the School of Business.

David G. Monical is vice-president for planning and governmental relations at Washburn University. He formerrly served the Kansas legislature as chief fiscal analyst for higher education.

The ability of organizations to operate effectively is highly dependent on the degree to which individuals' personal goals mesh with institutional aims.

Getting Individual and Organizational Goals to Match

David J. Berg

Ordinarily, a budget is thought of as a financial plan that brings anticipated expenditures into balance with anticipated revenues. There is, however, much more to a budget than this. In addition to balancing income and expense, the budget and its underlying rules should match the institution's goals with the desires of its clientele and should ensure that employees, in maximizing their own satisfactions, will be furthering the goals of the institution.

This chapter explores changes in management techniques that can help colleges and universities to operate more effectively and more efficiently—that is, with the least expenditure of resources to achieve institutional objectives (quantitative and qualitative goals) as completely as possible.

Effectiveness and efficiency are the aim of every individual and every organization. Each individual seeks to attain as much as possible of the satisfactions he or she desires at the least personal cost or sacrifice—that is, to maximize the satisfaction of personal

D. J. Berg, Gerald M. Skogley (Eds.). *Making the Budget Process Work.* New Directions for Higher Education, no. 52. San Francisco: Jossey-Bass, December 1985.

objectives. Each organization seeks to operate as efficiently as possible so that resources can be directed to the more complete accomplishment of existing goals or to the achievement of expanded goals.

The ability of organizations to operate effectively and efficiently is highly dependent on the degree to which the personal goals of individuals in organizations mesh with organizational objectives. Unless individuals within an organization have personal or collective incentives to work for organizational goals, they will not do so. Incentives may be individual or collective, positive or negative, monetary or nonmonetary. Individual incentives are usually more effective than collective incentives, although this may be less the case in universities than in most other organizations. Because they are not punitive and are less likely to create resentment, positive incentives are usually superior to negative incentives—the carrot is more effective than the stick. While monetary incentives, being more tangible, are generally considered superior to nonmonetary incentives, this may be less true in universities than elsewhere.

In the private sector, the usual methods of matching individual objectives to organizational objectives are to use market mechanisms to determine what the organization's clientele wants and what incentive budgeting and reward techniques will motivate employees to provide such a product effectively and efficiently. A voluminous literature supports the superiority of these practices over centralized planning approaches that ignore market strategies and attempt to regulate, punish, or exhort employees to correct nonperformance or noncompliance. The centralized planning approach cannot be successful for two reasons: First, it multiplies the administrative organization in order to force individual compliance with organizational objectives. In doing so, it removes authority and responsibility progressively further from an operational level and reduces the flexibility of the organization to react to changes in its goals and environment. Second, when individual incentives conflict with organizational goals, the individual will attempt to thwart certain goals; no management system can cope with this situation.

In behaving on an economic basis, people are almost never self-sacrificing idealists; the planner or budgeter who thinks efficiency and effectiveness can be achieved by multiplying rules and control mechanisms is engaged in self-delusion. People will work hardest to further their own objectives. Only by matching personal and organizational objectives can the organization hope to perform effectively.

Nonprofit institutions, and particularly the public sector,

provide a textbook example on poor practice in matching individual to organizational objectives. Efficiency and effectiveness are seldom rewarded and not infrequently are punished. Conversely, the failure to perform often leads to the unexamined allocation of increased resources. Multiple levels of detailed control often stifle innovation and creativity. Line item budget controls frustrate the most efficient combinations of the means of production. Pricing policy irrationally underprices what clientele are willing and able to pay for, or overprices when a price reduction might well increase revenue through higher volume.

Most of this undesirable practice arises from two misconceptions. One, the idea that efficiency and effectiveness can be enhanced by the imposition of additional levels and degrees of control and review, has been cited above. A related misconception is the idea that nonprofit enterprises cannot use incentive or market techniques. For many, the possibility of private ownership profits has become associated with the possibility of using the market and incentive methods. Yet for large organizations, even in the private sector, ownership returns are not, in themselves, the major incentive to performance. Every other market and incentive technique is, at least potentially, available for use in the nonprofit sector. While some may maintain that increased effectiveness and efficiency is dependent on transferring a function from the public to the private sector, the key element is probably not the profit or nonprofit status of the firm or organization but the degree to which it is free to use market and incentive techniques and, in fact, does so.

There are ample instances of poor quality production and inefficiency in the private economy, and it is significant that such examples are concentrated in relatively noncompetitive and highly regulated parts of that economy where market discipline has been distorted and the need to employ incentives has been minimized or the ability to do so restricted. One need not look far in the utility and transportation industries to find examples.

Models of effective and efficient performance in the nonprofit sector are more difficult to cite, but there are some. Certain religious and charitable organizations are likely to be highly congruent. The federal government has sometimes used a quasi-corporate form of organization to provide management flexibility and, at least in some instances, the result seems to have been superior performance.

If the reader will concede that there are some cases of ineffectiveness and inefficiency caused by market distortion and poor incentive structure in the profit sector, the point is made. Barriers to the use of market and incentive techniques by nonprofit organizations are structural and traditional, not intrinsic to the organizational form or the type of ownership.

The conformance of individual and organizational goals has two aspects. The organization's goals must be made to conform, as nearly as possible, to the goals of its clientele. This involves the creation or recognition of incentives for the organization to engage in a continuous process of measuring, testing, and assessing client demand. The goals of employees must be made to conform, as nearly as possible, to the organization's goals. This involves structuring the incentives of the individual employee in such a way that, by pursuing his or her own interest, the goals of the organization will be furthered. The first of these aspects suggests market techniques, such as the more perfect measurement of the incentives on the organization. The second aspect suggests internal incentive techniques, such as the structuring of incentives for individuals and subsets of the organization that will bring self-interest into alignment with organizational interests.

What practical application can be made of these ideas by colleges and universities? The rest of this chapter discusses a variety of ideas that are, in some degree, associated with incentive techniques defined above. Neither the list of ideas nor the discussion of each is represented as original or exhaustive. The purpose is simply to provide the reader with some specific ideas that may sharpen a perception of their utility and practicality, and to suggest useful modifications of budgetary rules and techniques.

Reading the Market

Higher education's clientele consists of students, governments, and nongovernmental individuals and organizations. The product of colleges and universities is instruction, research, and other products and services. For illustrative purposes, the following matrix gives a rough idea of the relative size for large universities of these markets in dollar terms.

	Instruction	Research	Other
Students	10%	n.a.	n.a.
Governments	30%	15%	5%
Others	5%	5%	30%

The 30 percent of revenues derived from sale of other services to the public and to students (in other than their instructional roles) consists mostly of hospital, auxiliary enterprise, and intercollegiate athletic activity, all of which are quite market sensitive. The important markets are student demand for instruction, the related government subsidies, and governmental and other research demand. Although research is now in progress on measuring governmental demand as unrelated to instructional subsidy, it is not treated here.

Historically, government subsidy of instruction has been closely related to student demand. Thus, the ability to improve the perception of student demand has potential effects on about half of total volume in large universities and much more in small institutions. Better measurement of student demand can result in improved resource allocation, thus enhancing total goal satisfaction, given available resources. It may also increase the available resources in two ways. Revenue may be increased by moving toward a combination of price and volume that yields a higher total. Relying on investor and consumer choice may reduce the costs associated with having planners and managers make choices on behalf of others.

Cost-Related Tuition

An important factor in improving the degree of satisfaction of client demand is a price schedule that reflects the relative cost of alternative options. Tuition and formula funding policies that reflect true cost more closely can improve the efficiency of resource allocation and thus improve client satisfaction and, perhaps, total revenues.

A tuition policy that relates tuition to cost by level and program, leaving room for exceptions based on the market and on desirable social and educational policy, may result in improved efficiency and effectiveness. Because demand elasticity is much greater, in general, for low cost than for higher cost programs, and because students in low cost programs, in general, pay a much greater proportion of their instructional costs than do students in higher cost programs, movement toward cost-related tuition will produce higher enrollments than would otherwise occur, higher total tuition revenues, and probably higher governmental subsidies. The practice of charging extremely variant percentages of instructional cost to different classes of students is a largely unexamined tradition that may be very costly as well as counterproductive in terms of institutional and public policy objectives.

Responsibility Center Budgeting

One method of encouraging effective, efficient performance is to make a unit's available budget visibly dependent on its output levels and to permit the unit to make its own decisions about resource allocation and pricing. There are examples in academe. The University of Pennsylvania, Washington University of St.

Louis, the University of Southern California, and Harvard are all at least partial practitioners of responsibility center budgeting.

In responsibility center budgeting, part or all of tuition and sponsored research revenues are returned to a unit in direct proportion to what is earned. The unit controls its own pricing policy and is, in turn, responsible for payment of all, or nearly all, of its costs. Surpluses remain with the unit; deficits must be made up by the unit in succeeding periods. The incentive to efficient production of what the market demands is obvious.

It should be noted that in some responsibility budgeting schemes the institution makes extramarket judgments about programs and finances them with a tax on market-related operations. This technique is not without problems. A fair internal pricing structure is required. While, in theory, a unit should have the freedom to purchase service within the university or outside it and should be able to choose between teaching a course itself or buying it from another unit, this may create problems at the university level. These problems are not insuperable, as experience at the above cited institutions shows.

Not every unit within a university need be on a responsibility budget basis for benefits to be realized. It is only necessary that the agreements with those units that are responsibility centers be such that the institution can continue adequate support for those that are not. It is here that an important advantage of incentive techniques is illustrated. Some of these techniques, at least, have the potential to produce behavior that benefits both the institution and all the parties within it. The zero-sum game of internal budgeting can be overcome. In the case of partial application of responsibility center budgeting, the responsibility centers can have an incentive to increase not only their own goal satisfaction but also the ability of the institution to support the aspirations of units not on a responsibility center basis.

Frequently, professional schools or other relatively self-contained units offer the possibility of experimentation with responsibility center budgeting. The detail work of moving to a comprehensive scheme of responsibility budgeting in a single step is a forbidding obstacle. Piecemeal experimentation is fully feasible. Serious budgeters interested in improving effectiveness and efficiency should be considering such experimentation.

Internal Sales and Pricing

To the extent that a unit's budget resources are not under its own control, that unit has no incentive to use the centrally controlled portion of its resources efficiently. A unit in possession of surplus or unused equipment supplies or space has no incentive to release those resources for use by another unit unless the possessor can realize some benefit from doing so. Resources will always be employed more efficiently if a price that approximates tradeoff value is attached to their use.

This suggests that it is desirable to allow interdepartmental sales of goods and services, to decentralize the responsibility for purchasing resources wherever there is a material result, and to operate service units on a chargeback basis wherever feasible. Where service, supplies, and equipment are not freely saleable among departments, they should be made so. Prices should be arrived at by free bargaining between the parties to the transaction. Note that equipment should be included in such a decontrol program to the extent permitted by law and contractual agreements. Decentralized control of telephone and computer budgets should be subject to special evaluation; a rise in expenditures subsequent to decontrol may be due to removal of a centralized control system that was constraining optimum information utility use.

Service units such as the general and chemical storehouses, vehicle rental, and scientific apparatus services should move steadily toward a system of charging for cost of goods and services, thus offering comparison with outside supply sources.

From a departmental standpoint, use of space in a centralized system is free once the space is assigned. No incentive exists to use the space efficiently; no incentive exists to release space that is surplus to departmental needs. Central space allocation is an interminable negotiation supported by attempts to arrive at normative space standards. Space allocation decisions could be decentralized through budgeting techniques. A space bank might be created offering one-time budgetary inducements to departments to release space. The rental value of space held by a department might be placed in the departmental budget and charged against it, at the same time allowing sales and trades of space. There may be situations where utility and space maintenance costs can be charged against decentralized budgets thus creating an incentive to efficiently use necessary space and to release surplus space.

There are many areas where internal sales and pricing can be introduced or extended. Implementing these market methods will lead to questions about make-or-buy choices and desirable standards of product or service purchase.

Make-or-Buy Decisions

A make-or-buy decision concerns whether to provide goods or services through internal organizational service units or to buy them from external suppliers. Incentives should be designed so that the manager will compare the cost of each option and select the choice that supplies the desired quantity at the lowest price. Where such incentives do not exist, misallocation and waste of resources will occur.

Where the decision is in the hands of the internal provider, the incentive to consider outside purchase is weakened and may be neutralized. This is effectively the case for many physical plant and service unit decisions in colleges and universities. Provided that minimal quality standards are met and the manager is spending his or her own money, it is desirable that make-or-buy decisions be made by the user of the goods or services. The goal is to have the person in authority make the decision and take the responsibility to pay for it.

Quality Standards

Meeting acceptable standards of output quality is part of the concept of effectiveness. Such standards are very rigorous for institutions of higher education. However, this goal may actually be impeded by use of unnecessarily high standards of input quality. If the choice of a standard for supplies, services, equipment, building design, or space allocation is higher than it need be to achieve acceptable output quality, the total effectiveness of the organization will be reduced as a result.

The best efforts to choose a minimal acceptable standard for resource inputs will be forthcoming only when the decision maker is confronted with a choice that has personal consequences. If money will be lost at the end of the year anyway, it may well be thrown away on unnecessarily luxurious expenditure. If there is no direct gain from the release of space or cost attached to retaining it, the manager will probably attempt to retain an uneconomically high space assignment standard to the detriment of the total organization.

Central control devices can be helpful here; some are essential. Centralized purchasing, bidding procedures, design review, review of personnel documents, all are useful, but they cannot be maximally effective without proper incentives for the decentralized operating unit and its manager. Here again we are confronted with the inability of direct control devices to manage a large organization effectively and efficiently. No central management can possibly prevail in a contest with decentralized units whose incentives cause them to strive to thwart, even inadvertently, the overall organizational goals.

Decentralized authority and responsibility, with clear organizational goals and the proper incentives to match them with unit goals, is the most desirable approach. In most colleges and universities, improvements in reversion practice and space costing offer the best possibilities for improved discrimination in quality of resource inputs.

Budgeting and Reversion Practice

The most common practice in public agency budgeting is end-of-year reversion of unspent balances to the next budgetary level and eventual pickup of most end-of-year overdrafts. In addition, in many systems, the failure to spend all of this year's budget is considered an argument for reducing next year's budget. Still worse is accepting an overdraft in itself as an argument for increasing the following year's budget. Anyone who has been involved in the budget activities of public agencies has a fund of horror stories about the inefficiency, hoarding, and outright waste caused by these practices. The reason is that these undesirable behaviors are not occasional, they are the norm, and it is hard to see how it could be otherwise given the incentives that the budget system provides for the unit managers. It is a rare manager, and probably a bad manager, who neglects to get any possible use out of existing resources, even if only to demonstrate that the budget was not excessive, when there are no personal or unit benefits for doing otherwise. This suggests two rules abut budget and reversion practice. Share end-of-year budget balances with the next lower operating level. Do not bail out overdrafts unless convinced that they resulted from initial budget errors.

Although end-of-year reversion remains the norm, nonreversion or balance sharing are in use in some institutions and appear to have had favorable results. Two problems deserve citation. There is a tendency to share balances only with academic units—an error since much of the inefficiency caused by reversion policy occurs in support and administrative units. The academic units are not benefited by overlooking the opportunity to correct that inefficiency. Where central support is unstable, it is desirable to use a balance sharing proportion that can be maintained from year to year. Similarly, exceptions to a no-bail-out policy should be very rare. Units must believe in the stability and permanency of a budget policy.

These budgetary practices are necessary, though not in themselves sufficient, to the strategy of matching individual and unit incentives to organizational goals.

Retrenchment Practice

Most of the common approaches to budget retrenchment are pernicious from an incentive standpoint. The worst is simply seizing unspent and contractually uncommitted balances. To do this equitably would require examination of literally every spending commitment in the organization. Hiring freezes and bans on travel and equipment expenditures are an example of this technique. The incentive created is to quick and uncritical commitment of resources early in a budget year.

Only slightly better is the formula retrenchment of budgets based on the type of expenditure planned. An illustration is the cutting of academic lines by one percentage, nonacademic personnel by another, and various types of nonpersonnel funds by still different percentages. The objection is that the severity of the cut may be very different depending solely on the mix of resources used in the unit—an irrelevant factor. Not only in retrenchment, but in general, unit management should be given maximum flexibility to select the most efficient combination of resources and should not be at hazard in doing so. To the manager who fears that this year's occurrence will repeat itself, the incentive is clear. Put everything possible into academic payroll regardless of whether doing so is efficient. Unless that is a goal of institutional policy, a perverse incentive is created.

A bit better is the single percentage reduction based on the unit's total budget. It avoids most of the negative internal incentives but it fails to distinguish the degree to which a unit has achieved centrality in supporting the organizational goals and thus weakens unit incentives to do so. It leaves unit management to achieve the goal in the most efficient possible way but provides no reward for past effectiveness or for relative value to the total enterprise.

Short of detailed internal analysis of each unit, the most effective approach to retrenchment, from the viewpoint of incentives, is a differential percentage reduction based on judgments about the centrality, effectiveness, and efficiency of the unit, not on the mix of expenditures within that unit. This leaves management to make the best of the situation, and they are the ones to best do that. It also sends valuable incentive messages about the unit's place in the organization's priorities.

Relaxation of line item controls is desirable at all times and is particularly desirable in times of retrenchment. Here, as elsewhere, it is a practical impossibility for central administrators to know the best method of varying resource inputs and that method will be very different in different units.

Relating Budgets to Performance Measures

Even though the performance of universities and their subunits is extremely difficult to measure or even approximate, the total dissociation of resource allocation and performance measurement would be the ultimate incentive mistake. Like it or not, the resources of an institution are a function of what its clientele perceive as its performance. They will continue to look for measures of performance and so must we. Unless we assess performance, institutional goals will be separated from the incentives offered to us by our clienteles. Unless we use that assessment in internal resource allocation, the incentives for our faculty and staff will be separated from the goals of the institution; either can be fatal.

This does not mean that resources should be rigidly tied to some simple enrollment measure; almost no planner or budgeter has ever believed that. Yet decision makers must use some criteria to allocate scarce resources. Those criteria, now and always, are going to involve performance measures, whether simple or sophisticated, objective or impressionistic. Improved effectiveness and efficiency rely on improved performance measurements.

There are at least two ways in which most schools could improve their performance measurement practices. We must find better methods of incorporating advising, both graduate and undergraduate, into our instructional measures. If budget success is predicated only on student credit hour output, a key incentive to quality performance is missing. Instead there is an incentive to minimal nonclassroom assistance and perhaps even to grade inflation. Measuring effort outside the classroom is difficult, but it should be noted that exactness is not required. Any agreed upon measure is better than no measure at all.

The measurement of research and creative activity is still trickier. Presumably it is usually done subjectively by provosts and deans. Are the standards similar? Some overt, quantifiable indices would improve the incentive situation. Can such measures be designed and agreed upon? Again, any agreed upon measures that make this phase of budget evaluation an overt process would be an improvement on the existing system in most institutions. Finally, are there other significant measures to which attention should be given in the interest of sending the proper signals about institutional priorities?

Venture Capital

It is ordinarily quite difficult to experiment with new products or markets without having the funding. This is particularly true in public agencies where the ability to accumulate flexible surpluses is usually severely limited if it exists at all. One of the roles appropriate to the central management of a decentralized, incentive-based enterprise is to act as merchant banker for venture entrepreneurs within the organization. The state, if it can be induced to do so, may also serve this function.

There are severe limitations on the ability of colleges and universities, particularly in the public sector, to provide venture capital. It has been argued that a venture capital fund will appear on the institution's books as a net balance at year-end closing, inviting recapture or budget reduction by the state. Other arguments have been of the "public agencies don't do that" type.

In spite of difficulties, it is likely that the availability of venture capital might encourage the sort of market experimentation and program innovation that simply does not occur under most present systems; this would be to the immense benefit of the organization in the long run. While the use of private funds may offer a solution in some cases, it is also true that state governments have been moving in the direction of a broader interpretation of fiscal policy wwith more consideration of long term implications. Well-designed venture capital schemes are more salable than they once were.

Prizes and Performance Bonuses

One of the most common incentive devices in the private economy is individual cash rewards for specified achievement. The method is not unknown in nonprofit enterprises. Many governmental units have experimented with such schemes particularly for executive level employees. Such plans deserve consideration. They must reward objectively measurable behavior that aids fulfillment of specific institutional objectives. They should not be dependent on the subjective judgment of supervisors or higher levels of management.

A related type of incentive plan is the suggestion system. It is reasonable to believe that line employees of colleges and universities are capable of suggesting many changes that could increase effectiveness and efficiency and of identifying many areas of waste and mismanagement. Schools that have no effective, widely publicized incentive system to bring forth such suggestions should certainly consider budgeting for such a system.

Replacement Incentives

Employees and decentralized managers will, in general, work to maximize effective achievement of organizational goals at minimal cost if there is something in it for them. Thus, if one would like to identify units or activities that should be cut back or eliminated, one should only expect aid in that effort if the person or unit involved can keep some of the potential saving. This is part of the reason for the commonly observed difficulty that public agencies have in stopping, or even reducing, any activity once it is started.

Why should a unit's management identify the possibility of reduction if only part of the surplus resources would remain when it can possibly retain all the surplus by noncooperation? The answer lies in pride of workmanship. People prefer to be engaged in valuable work; they want to do a good job. There must, however, be something to gain; the coin must have two sides. If offered a game of "heads I win, tails you lose," the rational person refuses to play and resists being forced. This has implications for both state and internal institutional planning and budgeting policy.

Public institutions should make every effort to convince state authorities that a policy of recapturing all, or nearly all, income growth is a self-defeating policy. Allowing the institution flexible use of a substantial part of the income it generates will tend to maximize that income for both parties. An opposite policy will minimize income in total and for both parties. If, in the future, programs or units must be reduced or eliminated, some of the resulting savings must be left with the institution or the incentives to carry out the reductions will not exist. The same admonitions apply to internal policies. If we simply say, "Tell me what you can cut and you will lose those resources," the result will be noncooperation and a continuing attempt to frustrate organizational planning.

A corollary is that sponsored or private funds must never appear to be merely replacement for existing funding. No sponsor will support a school if it appears that the result is a reduction in tax support. In a period of shrinking real state support, this may pose some delicate problems of public perception.

Sponsored Research Incentives

An obvious incentive to obtaining sponsored research agreements is the return of some substantial part of indirect cost recoveries to the department generating them. At many schools, such a system is already in effect, and where not in use, this system should be seriously considered. (The argument that indirect cost recoveries should be devoted to the overheads that generate them is irrelevant. By definition, the expenditures for overheads must be made; but these are unrestricted funds and, from a budget standpoint, it is the incentive effect that is important, not accounting neatness.)

This might be supplemented by a system of released time for proposal writing, research activity, and report preparation thereby making the departmental faculty collectively responsible for allocating available released time. The collective incentive would be to encourage departments to seek outside support wherever possible, to collegially improve the quality of research proposals, and to conserve available released time for meritorious cases where outside support is genuinely unobtainable.

Conclusion

Planning will be effective only as organizational incentives are made to match clientele demand and as internal incentives are made to match organizational goals. Individuals will work effectively and efficiently for organizational goals only if by doing so they can further their own goals. Admonition and coercion will not achieve this aim; only the design of proper incentive systems offers the possibility of achieving it. To ignore these considerations is to ensure ineffective planning and budgeting. To make long term planning successful, we must devote effort to the design and use of market and incentive techniques.

David J. Berg is assistant vice-president for
management planning and information services in the
University of Minnesota system.

Further sources of information are provided in this chapter.

Suggestions for Further Reading

David J. Berg

Probably the day is past when anyone motivated to read this volume would regard the budget process as simply an exercise in fiscal discipline involving mechanical procedures carried out by technicians. However, that day is not in the distant past, and such a view may be the mean toward which we tend to regress when pressures ease. The political nature of organizational budgets can never be overstressed; the budgetary functions of communicating organizational policy and stimulating desired organizational behavior are far more important than mere matching of outgo to income. Accordingly, reading to expand understanding of the budget process should stress the means by which these more policy-related aspects of the budget can be improved.

If there is a single essential source not only for budgeting but also for all fiscal functions in higher education, it is *College and University Business Administration* (NACUBO, 1982). Meisinger and Dubeck's book (1984) is a recent introductory volume written for faculty members and academic administrators new to the budgeting process. Although intended for the interested layman, it is sophisticated and well written, and seasoned budgeters may well profit

D. J. Berg, Gerald M. Skogley (Eds.). *Making the Budget Process Work.* New Directions for Higher Education, no. 52. San Francisco: Jossey-Bass, December 1985.

from it. Valuable particularly for its discussion of types of budgetary approach is Caruthers and Orwig's *Budgeting in Higher Education* (1979). Powell (1980) exhaustively discusses the processes of budget formation and follow through in nonprofit organizations—a volume for the professional written in textbook style.

Readers who want to pursue the issues raised by Gene Kemper in this volume should start with Dressel and Simon (1976), who emphasize intelligent resource allocation among academic departments as a sine qua non for effective budgeting. Also useful both from the standpoint of academic department budgeting and general budget modeling is Bleau (1982). The emphasis is on faculty flow models, although other sorts of faculty models are also cited and discussed.

An understanding of the politics of the budget process is a key to making it work, and Wildavsky (1979) is the classic work on the subject. Keller (1983) illustrates budget politics by example with rich case study material and also deals with the introduction of a new emphasis on strategic planning concepts in the management of American higher education. A delightful discussion of budgeting ploys is found in Chapter Ten of Anthony and Herzlinger (1975), a very readable book that has much else to offer. Mingle (1981) and Hyatt, Shulman, and Santiago (1984) are useful case study collections that touch on political forces affecting reallocation budgets.

The importance of an effective nexus between planning and budgeting is commonplace today. One suspects, however, that it is often affirmed in theory and violated in practice. It cannot be stated too often that, unless planning drives budgeting, formal planning is a waste of time and resources. A thoughtful collection of essays on how the linkage can be achieved and maintained is found in Micek (1980). As Green and Monical point out in this volume, strategic planning, properly practiced, can be a factor in making the budget an instrument of the plan. The reader who wants to delve deeper into that possibility should consult, first, Merson and Qualls (1979) and then Green, Naggar, and Ruch (1979).

Of great interest currently are discussions of incentive versus control budgeting, or to put it more precisely, the creation of incentive structures in the budget that are a support rather than an obstacle to efficient performance that supports the planning. While some of this discussion has to do with excessive or counterproductive controls by the political overhead, most such problems have their analogs in internal budget practices. Brenda Albright's chapter in this volume addresses questions of how the budget can be used to promote quality output of instruction and research. The idea of positive incentives in preference to sanctions is still relatively novel in nonprofit and public sector budgeting. A convenient entry to this literature is four papers: Hoenack and others (1974), Hoenack (1977), Zemsky, Porter, and Odel (1978), and Strauss and Salamon (1979). Hoenack also discusses the most recent research in Wilson (1984). Hyatt and Santiago (1984) is a thought-provoking casebook. One of the most interesting specific techniques is differentiated, cost-related tuition schedules. Hoenack and Weiler (1975) remains the key reference in that area.

Although budgetary modeling has a considerable history, it is doubtful that modeling techniques are widely used. The pain of the budget process can be greatly mitigated and its effectiveness increased by the judicious use of appropriate and well-designed models. Wyatt, Emery, and Landis (1979) is a good start and Hopkins and Massy (1981) is currently the definitive work and is written in such a way as to be useful to readers through a considerable range of mathematical sophistication.

Anthony, R. N., and Herzlinger, R. E. *Management Control in Nonprofit Organizations.* Homewood, Ill.: Richard D. Irwin, 1975.

Bleau, B. L. "Faculty Planning Models: A Review of the Literature." *Journal of Higher Education,* 1982, *53* (2), 195–206.

Caruthers, J. K., and Orwig, M. *Budgeting in Higher Education.* Washington, D.C.: American Association of Higher Education, 1979.

Dressel, P., and Simon, L. A. K. (eds.). *Allocating Resources Among Departments.* New Directions for Institutional Research, no. 11 San Francisco, Calif.: Jossey-Bass, 1976.

Green, J. L., Jr., Naggar, D. P., and Ruch, R. S. *Strategic Planning and Budgeting for Higher Education.* La Jolla, Calif.: J. L. Green and Associates, 1979.

Hoenack, S. A., and Weiler, W. C. "Cost Related Tuition Policies and University Enrollments." *Journal of Human Resources,* 1975, *10,* 332–360.

Hoenack, S. A. "Direct and Incentive Planning Within a University." *Socio-Economic Planning Sciences,* 1977, *11,* 191–204.

Hoenack, S. A., and others. "University Planning, Decentralization, and Resource Allocation." *Socio-Economic Planning Sciences,* 1974, *8,* 257–272.

Hopkins, D. S. P., and Massy, W. F. *Planning Models for Colleges and Universities.* Stanford, Calif.: Stanford University Press, 1981.

82

Hyatt, J. A., and Santiago, A. A. *Incentives and Disincentives for Effective Management.* Washington, D.C.: National Association of College and University Business Officers, 1984.

Hyatt, J. A., Shulman, C. H., and Santiago, A. A. *Reallocation: Strategies for Effective Resource Management.* Washington, D.C.: National Association of College and University Business Officers, 1984.

Keller, G. *Academic Strategy.* Baltimore, Md.: The Johns Hopkins University Press, 1983.

Meisinger, R. J., and Dubeck, L. W. *College and University Budgeting.* Washington, D.C.: National Association of College and University Business Officers, 1984.

Merson, J. C., and Qualls, R. L. *Strategic Planning for Colleges and Universities.* San Antonio, Tex.: Trinity University Press, 1979.

Micek, S. S. (ed.). *Integrating Academic Planning and Budgeting in a Rapidly Changing Environment: Process and Technical Issues.* Boulder, Colo.: National Center for Higher Education Management Systems, 1980.

Mingle, J. R., and Associates. *Challenges of Retrenchment: Strategies for Consolidating Programs, Cutting Costs, and Reallocating Resources.* San Francisco, Calif.: Jossey-Bass, 1981.

National Association of College and University Business Officers (NACUBO). *College and University Business Administration.* (4th ed.) Washington, D.C.: NACUBO, 1982.

Powell, R. M. *Budgetary Control Procedures for Institutions.* Notre Dame, Ind.: University of Notre Dame Press, 1980.

Strauss, J. C., and Salamon, L. D. "Using Financial Incentives in Academic Planning and Management." *Business Officer,* 1979, *13,* 14-17.

Wildavsky, A. *The Politics of the Budgetary Process.* (3rd ed.) Boston, Mass.: Little, Brown & Co., 1979.

Wilson, R. A. (ed.). *Administering and Managing the Finances of Colleges and Universities.* (Topical Paper No. 23) Tucson: University of Arizona Center for the Study of Higher Education, 1984.

Wyatt, J. B., Emery, J. C., and Landis, C. P. (eds.). *Financial Planning Models: Concepts and Case Studies in Colleges and Universities.* Princeton, N.J.: EDUCOM, 1979.

Zemsky, R., Porter, R., and Odel, L. P. "Decentralized Planning Responsibility." *Educational Record,* 1978, *59,* 229-253.

David J. Berg is assistant vice-president for management planning and information services in the University of Minnesota system.

Index

STATEMENT OF OWNERSHIP, MANAGEMENT, AND CIRCULATION

New Directions for
Higher Education

Quarterly

Jossey-Bass Inc., Publishers, 433 California St., San Francisco, CA 94104

433 California St. San Francisco (SF County) CA 94104

433 California St. San Francisco (SF County) CA 94104

Jossey-Bass Inc. Publishers 433 California St., San Francisco, CA 94104

Martin Kramer, 2857 Shasta Rd. Berkeley, CA 94708

Allan Jossey-Bass, Jossey-Bass Publishers, 433 California St., S.F. CA 94104

Full Name	Complete Mailing Address
Jossey-Bass Inc. Publishers	433 California St., S.F., CA 94104

For names and addresses of stockholders, See attached list.

Full Name	Complete Mailing Address
Same as 11	

	Average No. Copies Each Issue During Preceding 12 Months	Actual No. Copies of Single Issue Published Nearest to Filing Date
a. Total No. Copies (Net Press Run)	1922	2043
b. Paid and/or Requested Circulation		
(1) Sales Through Dealers	343	34
(2) Mail Subscription	1364	1264
c. Total Paid and/or Requested Circulation	1706	1298
d. Free Distribution by Mail	105	105
e. Free Distribution Outside the Mail	1811	1403
f. Total Free Distribution	63	63
g. Total Distribution	0	0
h. Copies Not Distributed	1922	2043
i. Total		

I certify that all statements made by me above are correct and complete.